Audit Report

OIG-14-007

Audit of the Community Development Financial Institutions
Fund's Fiscal Years 2013 and 2012 Financial Statements

December 13, 2013

Office of
Inspector General

Department of the Treasury

DEPARTMENT OF THE TREASURY
WASHINGTON, D.C. 20220

December 13, 2013

**MEMORANDUM FOR DONNA J. GAMBRELL, DIRECTOR
COMMUNITY DEVELOPMENT FINANCIAL
INSTITUTIONS FUND**

FROM: Michael Fitzgerald
Director, Financial Audit

SUBJECT: Audit of the Community Development Financial Institutions
Fund's Fiscal Years 2013 and 2012 Financial Statements

I am pleased to transmit the attached audited Community Development Financial
Institutions Fund (CDFI Fund) financial statements for fiscal years 2013 and 2012.
Under a contract monitored by the Office of Inspector General, KPMG LLP (KPMG),
an independent certified public accounting firm, performed an audit of the CDFI
Fund's statements of financial position as of September 30, 2013 and 2012 and
the related statements of operations and changes in net position and cash flows for
the years then ended. The contract required that the audit be performed in
accordance with generally accepted government auditing standards and Office of
Management and Budget Bulletin No. 14-02, *Audit Requirements for Federal
Financial Statements.*

The following reports, prepared by KPMG, are incorporated in the attachment:

- Independent Auditors' Report;
- Independent Auditors' Report on Internal Control Over Financial Reporting;
  and
- Independent Auditors' Report on Compliance and Other Matters

In its audit, KPMG found:

- the financial statements were fairly presented, in all material respects, in
  accordance with U.S. generally accepted accounting principles;
- no deficiencies in internal control over financial reporting that are considered
  material weaknesses; and
- no instances of reportable noncompliance with laws and regulations tested.

KPMG also issued a management letter dated December 12, 2013, discussing a
matter involving internal control that was identified during the audit but was not
required to be included in the auditors' reports. This letter will be transmitted
separately.

In connection with the contract, we reviewed KPMG's reports and related documentation and inquired of its representatives. Our review, as differentiated from an audit performed in accordance with generally accepted government auditing standards, was not intended to enable us to express, and we do not express, an opinion on the CDFI Fund's financial statements or conclusions about the effectiveness of internal control or compliance with laws and regulations. KPMG is responsible for the attached auditors' reports dated December 12, 2013, and the conclusions expressed in the reports. However, our review disclosed no instances where KPMG did not comply, in all material respects, with generally accepted government auditing standards.

Should you have any questions, please contact me at (202) 927-5789, or a member of your staff may contact Catherine Yi, Manager, Financial Audit, at (202) 927-5591.

Attachment

Community Development Financial Institutions Fund

United States Department of the Treasury

Agency Financial Report
FY 2013

Table of Contents

Message from the Director

I am pleased to present the fiscal year (FY) 2013 Agency Financial Report for the U.S. Department of the Treasury's Community Development Financial Institutions Fund (CDFI Fund). In addition to all that we have achieved this fiscal year, we continue to demonstrate our commitment to sound financial management, having obtained an unmodified opinion on our financial statements from independent auditors with no material weaknesses.

I would like to thank the staff of the CDFI Fund for their exceptional dedication and hard work throughout the fiscal year. Without them, none of the accomplishments highlighted in this report would have been possible.

In September 2013, the CDFI Fund announced the FY 2013 monetary awards for the Community Development Financial Institutions Program (CDFI Program) and the Native American CDFI Assistance Program (NACA Program). The awards totaled $185 million — $172.6 million for the CDFI Program (including $22.3 million in awards through the Healthy Food Financing Initiative) and nearly $12.4 million for NACA Program — and were made to 236 organizations serving low-income and Native communities across the country. The CDFI Fund received a combined total of 483 applications requesting a combined total of over $511 million in requests under the CDFI Program and NACA Program.

The demand for our Bank Enterprise Award (BEA) Program, which provides awards to Federal Deposit Insurance Corporation (FDIC)-insured banks and thrifts that increase their investments in CDFIs, community development lending, investments, and service-related activities, also remains strong. The CDFI Fund announced the 2012 BEA awardees during the first quarter of FY 2013. Fifty-nine (59) FDIC-insured institutions were selected to receive approximately $18 million in FY 2012 BEA Program awards. For the FY 2013 funding round of the program, we received 98 applications requesting more than $91 million in awards.

In FY 2013, the CDFI Fund released the interim rule for the CDFI Bond Guarantee Program and, in June 2013, we opened the program's inaugural round with the posting of the application materials and the publication of the first Notice of Guarantee Availability (NOGA). The CDFI Bond Guarantee Program has the potential to transform the community development finance industry by injecting new and substantial capital into our nation's most distressed communities. In September 2013, we announced the approval of term sheets for $325 million in bonds through the program.

Also, in the second quarter of FY 2013, we selected 85 Community Development Entities to receive tax credit authority allocations, totaling $3.5 billion, through the calendar year (CY) 2012 round of the New Markets Tax Credit Program (NMTC Program). The CDFI Fund has now awarded $36.5 billion in tax credit authority through ten rounds of the program. In CY 2012, the CDFI Fund received 282 applications requesting an aggregate total over $21.9 billion in NMTC allocation authority.

In addition to these programmatic accomplishments, there were a number of other important achievements that I would like to highlight.

Throughout FY 2013, the CDFI Fund continued its efforts to strengthen the oversight of award recipients by:

- reallocating existing resources to hire additional staff for the programs and certification and compliance management business units;

- developing a risk-based approach to compliance management with processes that assess risks associated with a combination of institutional factors and previous awardee compliance history; and
- re-instituting compliance site visits and desk audits of awardees with apparent and pervasive problems in meeting performance goals in their Assistance Agreements.

In addition, to further strengthen compliance management, the CDFI Fund implemented a major initiative requiring all certified CDFIs whose original or most recent certification was more than three years old to apply for recertification. By the end of FY 2013, the CDFI Fund had recertified 425 CDFIs and certified 76 new CDFIs. The total number of certified CDFIs as of the end of FY 2013 was 811.

Finally, the CDFI Fund has also been at work on a new report to assess the state of access to capital and credit in Native American, Alaskan Native and Native Hawaiian communities (Native Communities). We gathered public comments on the focus and methodology of the proposed report from November 2012 until February 2013. I am pleased to share that researchers are in place and have begun their important work on this needed report. The report will provide policy-makers, Tribal governments, Tribal community organizations, and economic development practitioners with detailed analysis and quantitative research that can lead to actionable recommendations for improving access to capital and credit in Native Communities.

As all these examples clearly demonstrate, the CDFI Fund has continued to succeed in its mission to generate economic opportunity in communities where such opportunity is needed most.

Donna J. Gambrell

Director
Community Development Financial Institutions Fund
December 12, 2013

Community Development Financial Institutions Fund Overview

Overview

In 1994, the Community Development Financial Institutions Fund (CDFI Fund) was created for the purpose of promoting economic revitalization and community development through investment in and assistance to Community Development Financial Institutions (CDFIs). Since 1996, the CDFI Fund has administered the Community Development Financial Institutions Program (CDFI Program) and the Bank Enterprise Award Program (BEA Program) to help build the capacity of CDFIs, increase investment in CDFIs, and increase community development lending, investments, and service-related activities in distressed communities, respectively. The CDFI Fund's role in promoting community and economic development was expanded in FY 2001 when the Secretary of the Treasury delegated to the CDFI Fund the responsibility of administering the New Markets Tax Credit Program (NMTC Program). The breadth and depth of the CDFI Fund's reach was further expanded in FY 2008, with the enactment of legislation that created the Financial Education and Counseling Pilot Program (FEC Pilot Program) and the enactment of legislation that created the Capital Magnet Fund (CMF), both of which were implemented in FY 2010; and again in FY 2010 with the enactment of legislation that created the CDFI Bond Guarantee Program for which the CDFI Fund began implementation planning in FY 2011.

Since its creation in 1994, the CDFI Fund has awarded more than $1.9 billion to CDFIs, community development organizations, and financial institutions through the CDFI Program, the BEA Program, and the Native Initiatives, which includes the Native American CDFI Assistance Program (NACA Program). In addition, the CDFI Fund has allocated $36.5 billion in tax credit authority to Community Development Entities (CDEs) through the NMTC Program. In FY 2013, the CDFI Fund obligated $325 million for guarantees through the CDFI Bond Guarantee Program.

Authorizing Legislation

The CDFI Fund was established as a bipartisan initiative under the Riegle Community Development and Regulatory Improvement Act of 1994, which also authorized the CDFI Program and BEA Program. The NMTC Program was authorized through the Community Renewal Tax Relief Act of 2000. The FEC Pilot Program and the CMF were authorized through the Housing and Economic Recovery Act of 2008. The CDFI Bond Guarantee Program was authorized as part of the Small Business Jobs Act of 2010.

CDFI Fund's Vision and Mission

The CDFI Fund's vision is to economically empower America's underserved and distressed communities. Its mission is to increase economic opportunity and promote community development investments for underserved populations and in distressed communities in the United States. The CDFI Fund achieves its purpose by promoting access to capital and local economic growth through the following programs:

Community Development Financial Institutions Program, which provides Financial Assistance awards to institutions that are certified as CDFIs and Technical Assistance grants to certified CDFIs and entities that will become certified as CDFIs within two years in order to sustain and expand their services and to build their technical capacity;

Native Initiatives, which includes the Native American CDFI Assistance Program (NACA Program); this program provides Financial Assistance and Technical Assistance awards to CDFIs serving Native American, Alaskan Native and Native Hawaiian communities (Native Communities) to sustain and expand their services and to build their technical capacity; and training opportunities for Native CDFIs available as part of the CDFI Fund's Capacity Building Initiative;

New Markets Tax Credit Program, which provides tax credit allocation authority to certified Community Development Entities (CDEs), enabling investors to claim tax credits against their federal income taxes. The CDEs in turn use the capital raised to make investments in low-income communities;

Bank Enterprise Award Program, which provides monetary awards to federally insured banks and thrifts for increasing investments in low-income communities and/or CDFIs;

CDFI Bond Guarantee Program, which guarantees the full amount of bonds issued to support CDFIs that make investments for eligible community or economic development purposes. These bonds support CDFI lending and investment by providing a source of long-term capital;

Capital Magnet Fund, which provided grants for CDFIs and other non-profits to finance the development, rehabilitation, and purchase of affordable housing for low-income people; and

Financial Education and Counseling Pilot Program, which provided financial assistance awards to enable certified CDFIs and other eligible organizations to deliver a variety of financial education and counseling services to prospective homebuyers.

What is a CDFI?

Providing access to affordable financial products and services in underserved communities is a vital part of the CDFI Fund's mission. By building the capacity of a nation-wide network of specialized financial institutions serving economically distressed communities, low-income people are empowered to enter the financial mainstream. The community-based organizations that make this possible are called Community Development Financial Institutions—or CDFIs—and they are dedicated to serving market niches that are often underserved by traditional financial institutions. The first step to utilizing many of the CDFI Fund's programs is CDFI Certification. For example, only financial institutions certified by the CDFI Fund can receive Financial Assistance awards through the CDFI Program and the NACA Program. Technical Assistance awards are available through both programs to certified CDFIs and entities that propose to become certified CDFIs.

CDFIs provide a unique and wide range of financial products and services that help their customers build wealth and achieve the goal of participating in the ownership society. While the types of products made available are generally similar to those provided by mainstream financial institutions (such as mortgage financing for low-income and first-time homebuyers, small business lending, and lending for community facilities), CDFIs often lend to and make equity investments in markets that may not be served by mainstream financial institutions. In addition, CDFIs may offer rates and terms that are more flexible to low-income borrowers and small businesses. CDFIs also provide services that help ensure that credit is used effectively, such as technical assistance to small businesses, and home buying and credit counseling to

6

consumers. CDFIs include depository institutions, such as community development banks and credit unions, and non-depository institutions, such as loan funds and venture capital funds.

CDFI Customers

CDFIs serve a wide range of customers, including (among others):

- Small business owners who provide employment opportunities and needed services to disadvantaged communities;

- Affordable housing developers who construct and rehabilitate homes in low-income communities;

- Community facilities used to provide child care, health care, education, and social services in underserved communities;

- Commercial real estate developers who finance the acquisition, construction, or rehabilitation of retail, office, industrial, and community facility space in low-income communities; and

- Individuals who are provided affordable banking services including checking and savings accounts, alternatives to predatory financial companies, and mortgages and other kinds of loans.

Certification of Community Development Financial Institutions and Community Development Entities

CDFI certification is a designation conferred by the CDFI Fund. An organization must meet the following seven statutory and regulatory criteria:

1) Be a legal entity;

2) Have a primary mission of promoting community development;

3) Serve principally an investment area or targeted population;

4) Be an insured depository institution, or otherwise have the offering of financial products and services as its predominant business activity;

5) Provide development services (such as technical assistance or counseling) in conjunction with its financing activity;

6) Maintain accountability to its target market; and

7) Be a non-governmental entity and not be controlled by any governmental entities.

CDFI certification is a requirement for accessing Financial Assistance awards through the CDFI Program and the NACA Program, and certain benefits through the BEA Program. In addition, organizations pursue CDFI certification in order to leverage CDFI funding from non-Federal sources such as banks, foundations, state and local governments. CDFI certification is also required of Eligible CDFIs in order to borrow Bond Loans through the CDFI Bond Guarantee Program.

The certification of organizations as CDFIs has been a CDFI Fund function since its inception. During FY 2013, the CDFI Fund undertook a major effort to recertify every CDFI whose original or most recent certification had passed its three-year term. The recertification initiative was announced to the CDFI community on February 4, 2013; as a result of that announcement, more than 500 CDFIs applied for recertification by April 8, 2013 or upon the expiration of three-year terms in subsequent months. By the end of FY 2013, the CDFI Fund had recertified 425 CDFIs and certified 76 new CDFIs. The total number of certified CDFIs as of the end of FY 2013 was 811. CDFIs are headquartered in all 50 states, the District of Columbia, Guam, Puerto Rico, and the U.S. Virgin Islands.

A Community Development Entity (CDE) is a domestic corporation or partnership that is an intermediary vehicle for the provision of loans, investments, or financial counseling in low-income communities through the NMTC Program. To be certified as a CDE, organizations must demonstrate a primary mission of serving low-income communities and low-income people, and must demonstrate that they are accountable (through representation on a governing board or advisory board) to residents of low-income communities. CDEs are certified as such by the CDFI Fund and are eligible to apply for allocations of tax credit authority through the NMTC Program.

Many CDEs create multiple subsidiary CDEs to own specific assets or classes of assets; as a result, 481 new CDEs were certified in FY 2013. Benefits of CDE certification include being able to: (1) apply to the CDFI Fund to receive an allocation of NMTC authority to offer to investors in exchange for equity investments in the CDE and/or its subsidiaries; or (2) receive loans or investments from other CDEs that have received NMTC allocations. As of September 30, 2013, the total number of certified CDEs was 6,359. This compares to 5,878 CDEs that were certified as of the end of FY 2012. CDEs are headquartered in 49 states, the District of Columbia, Puerto Rico, and the U.S. Virgin Islands.

Breakdown of Types of Certified CDFIs

There are four main types of CDFIs and each provides a different mix of products geared to reach specific customers:

- *Community development banks, thrifts and bank holding companies* are regulated for-profit corporations that provide capital to rebuild economically distressed communities through targeted lending and investment;
- *Community development credit unions* are regulated non-profit cooperatives owned by members that promote ownership of assets and savings and provide affordable credit and retail financial services to low-income people;
- *Community development loan funds* (usually non-profits) provide financing and development services to businesses, organizations and individuals in low-income urban and rural areas and can be further categorized based on the type of client served: micro-enterprise, small business, housing, and community service organizations; and
- *Community development venture capital funds* include both for-profit and non-profit organizations that provide equity and debt-with-equity features for businesses in distressed communities.

CDFI Fund's Key Performance Results for FY 2013

The CDFI Fund's key performance results for FY 2013 are provided below with CDFI Fund-wide summary performance results in the top panel, and selected program-level results in the bottom panel. Please note that this information summarizes awardees' performance results for program year 2012. These performance measures were newly adopted in FY 2012 so there was little baseline information for projecting targets.

CDFI Program awardees and NMTC Program allocatees helped provide funds for projects that created or maintained 50,353 jobs. In addition, CDFI Program awardees and NMTC Program allocatees helped finance 7,161 businesses, and real estate loans financed 26,391 affordable housing units, including 22,519 rental units and 3,872 owner units.

In FY 2013, CDFI Program awardees reported originating 24,285 loans or investments totaling nearly $1.9 billion, based on their portfolio of activities in 2012.

NMTC Program allocatees made $4.8 billion of loans and investments in Qualified Active Low-Income Community Businesses, with 78.5 percent of the dollars invested in loans and investments in severely distressed communities.

CDFI Fund's Key Performance Measures for FY 2013
(Based on Program Activities Reported in 2012)

	2012 Baseline	2013 Targets	2013 Results
CDFI FUND-WIDE SUMMARY RESULTS:			
All Affordable Housing Units Financed	**27,433**	**24,000**	26,391
Rental Units	22,445		22,519
Owner Units	4,988		3,872
All Businesses Financed[1]	**4,680**	**5,000**	7,161
All Jobs at End of Reporting Period	**57,023**	**50,000**	50,353
PROGRAM-LEVEL RESULTS:			
CDFI Program: Lending and Investing Activity:			
Amount of Total Loans/Investments Originated ($millions)	$1,298	$1,200	$1,978
Number of Total Loans/Investments Originated	17,547	16,900	24,285
NMTC Program: Lending and Investing Activity:			
Total Qualified Low-Income Community Investments ($millions)	$5,518	$4,000	$4,839
Percent of NMTC Program Loans/Investments in Severely Distressed Communities[2]	70.6%	70.5%	78.54%

Compliance Monitoring and Evaluation

The CDFI Fund is committed to a vision for compliance management which is informed not only by the results of CDFI Fund Program reporting requirements, but also by risk analysis that highlights to the CDFI Fund awardees and allocatees whose financial wherewithal requires special attention from the CDFI Fund's compliance management staff.

---

[1] This number reflects netting out businesses that received more than one loan.
[2] "Severely distressed" communities include Census tracts with poverty rates above 30 percent; or median family incomes below 60 percent of the metropolitan or state median; or unemployment rates greater than 1.5 times the national average.

In FY 2013, the CDFI Fund took several important steps in order to ensure that its compliance management function will be a robust effort that includes the following:

Establishing a 90-day performance metric for reviewing compliance reports from awardees and allocatees; Developing a risk-based scorecard to be implemented in FY 2014. The scorecard will allow the CDFI Fund to focus attention on those organizations deemed to be in a higher risk category.

Reactivated site visits and desk reviews of CDFIs and CDEs, with 22 site visits and 15 desk reviews conducted during FY 2013. The site visits and desk reviews have been extremely useful in enabling the CDFI Fund to evaluate issues facing awardees with particular compliance reporting deficiencies.

As noted elsewhere in this document, the CDFI Fund is continuing efforts to procure an Awards Management Information System (AMIS) in FY 2014, with anticipated deployment in FY 2015. AMIS will replace legacy business systems used by the CDFI Fund for its business processes. For compliance management, AMIS will electronically perform compliance testing for Performance Goals and Measures required by assistance and allocation agreements and provide reports of exceptions on a timely basis both to CDFI Fund compliance staff and to awardees and allocatees.

When AMIS is fully implemented, electronic compliance testing will enable CDFI Fund compliance staff to perform more thorough compliance analysis, through expanded desk reviews of awardee financial and programmatic data and on-site reviews of awardee accomplishments.

Allocation of CDFI Fund Funding

The CDFI Fund's appropriations comprise program funds and administrative funds. Program funds are used for program awards (such as grants, loans, deposits, equity investments, and capacity building / training contracts); administrative funds are used to cover the costs to administer all programs, including the NMTC Program. As NMTC allocations are not monetary awards, they are not reflected in the chart below. NMTC Program administrative expenses are included in the administration costs below.

In FY 2013, the CDFI Fund's budgetary allocation of $209.4 million in appropriated funds are as follows:

Funding Allocation
(Amounts in Millions)

	FY 2013	FY 2012
Amounts Funded		
CDFI Program	$159.2	$168.0
BEA Program	17.0	18.0
Native Initiatives	11.4	12.0
NMTC Program & Administrative Costs	21.8	23.0
Total Amounts Funded	209.4	221.0
Less Amounts Not Obligated*	24.8	31.7
Total Funding Used	**$184.6**	**$189.3**

* In FY 2012, the CDFI Fund carried over $31.7 million which included $7.4 million from the CDFI Program (this includes unobligated balances from HFFI and the Subsidies for Direct Loans), $18.0

million from the BEA Program, $0.1 million from the NACA Program, and $6.2 million for Program Administration.

In FY 2013, the CDFI Fund carried over $24.8 million which included $ 1.3 million from the CDFI Program (this includes unobligated balances from HFFI and the Subsidies for Direct Loans), $17.0 million from the BEA Program, $0.6 million from the NACA Program, and $5.9 million for Program Administration.

Percent of Amounts Funded in FY 2013

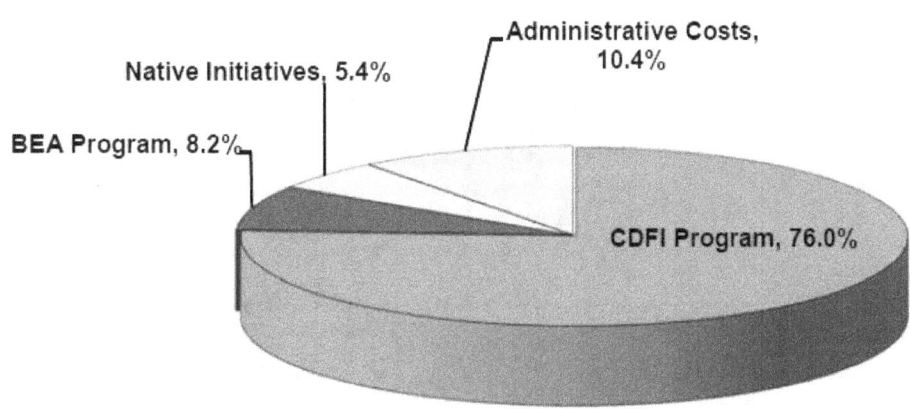

Sources of Funding

Congress appropriates funding annually to the CDFI Fund; each appropriation can be used over two fiscal years. Appropriations include fiscal year budget authority, and any unobligated funds from the prior year may be carried over. The annual appropriation amount includes borrowing authority to make loans.

Sources of CDFI Fund Funding
(Amounts in Millions)

	FY 2013	FY 2012
Budgetary Appropriations	$209.4	$221.0
Prior Year Amounts Deobligated, Used to Fund Current Year Obligations	6.6	2.5
Carryover from Prior Year	31.7	35.5
Spending Authority from Offsetting Collections	0.2	0.0
No-Year Funds	4.0	4.0
Borrowing Authority Used	9.8	4.2
Total Sources of Funds	**$261.7**	**$267.2**

Note: The above amounts do not include credit subsidy re-estimates.

Organization of the CDFI Fund

The CDFI Fund's organizational structure consists of offices managed by the following: Director; Deputy Director; Legislative and External Affairs Manager; Legal Counsel; Chief Financial Officer; CDFI and Native Programs Manager; Operations Manager; NMTC and BEA Programs Manager; Certification,

Compliance Monitoring, and Evaluation Manager; Financial Strategies and Research Manager; Training and Outreach Manager; Chief Information Officer; and CDFI Bond Guarantee Program Manager. The organization chart of the CDFI Fund is shown below.

Community Development Financial Institutions Fund
Organizational Chart
September 2013

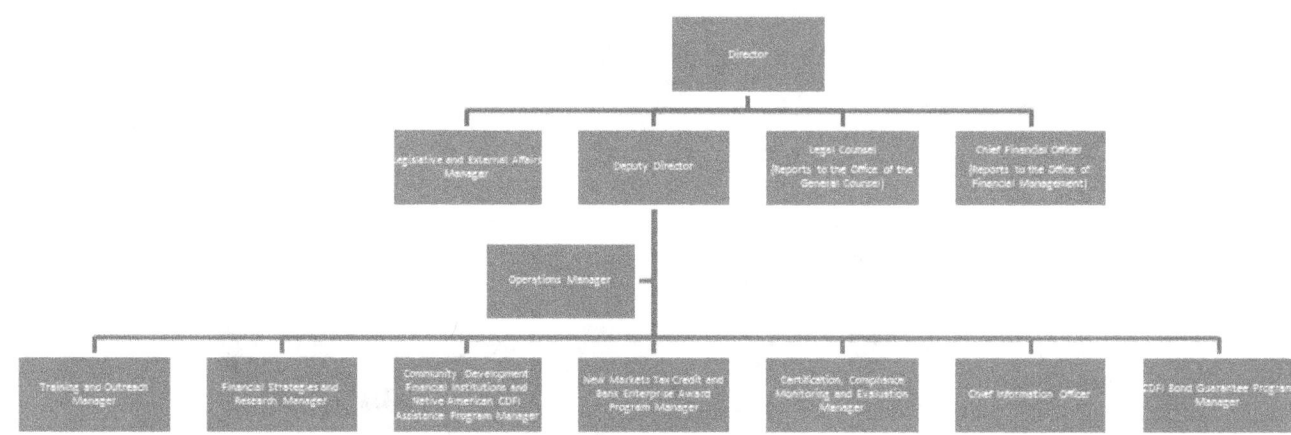

Program Discussion and Analysis

Community Development Financial Institutions Program

Through the Community Development Financial Institutions Program (CDFI Program), the CDFI Fund uses Federal resources to invest in and build the capacity of CDFIs to serve low-income people and communities lacking adequate access to affordable financial products and services. The CDFI Program provides monetary awards for Financial Assistance (FA) and Technical Assistance (TA). CDFIs use FA awards to further goals such as:

- Economic development (job creation, business development, and commercial real estate development);

- Affordable housing (housing development and homeownership); and

- Community development financial services (provision of basic banking services and financial literacy training to underserved communities).

In FY 2013, the CDFI Program announced awards totaling $172.6 million to CDFIs - $150.3 million in CDFI Fund Program awards and $22.3 million in Healthy Food Financing Initiative (HFFI) awards. The CDFI Program used $9.3 million of the FY 2012 funds and $162.5 million of the FY 2013 funds for $171.8 million in FY 2013 awards.[1]

Financial Assistance

The CDFI Program consists of two components, FA awards and TA awards. The FA component is by far the most subscribed and consists of two categories: Category 1 – Small and Emerging CDFI Assistance (SECA); and Category 2 – Core. Through the CDFI Program, the CDFI Fund invests in CDFIs that provide financing and related services to communities and populations lacking access to credit, capital, and financial services.

Applicants to the CDFI Program must demonstrate they have the financial and managerial capacity to make significant impact in the communities they serve. Applicants must: 1) be able to provide affordable and appropriate financial products and services; 2) be a viable financial institution; 3) be able to use CDFI Program awards effectively; and 4) have the ability to leverage their awards with non-Federal funding.

The CDFI Program makes FA awards in the form of equity investments, loans, deposits, and grants; the CDFI is required to match its FA award dollar-for-dollar with non-Federal funds of the same type as the award itself. This requirement enables CDFIs to leverage private capital to meet the demand for

---

[1] Final FY 2013 awards were $0.2 million less than announced due to lower obligations actually incurred under the terms of the final award agreements.

13

affordable financial products and services, including loans, investments, training, and basic financial services such as checking or savings accounts, in economically distressed communities.

FY 2013 FA Awards

In FY 2013, the Financial Assistance Program received eligible applications from 303 organizations, requesting a $395.5 million in FA awards, including 86 SECA applicants requesting $48.8 million and 217 Core applicants seeking $346.7 million.

The CDFI Fund awarded a total of $146.7 million to 148 organizations in FY 2013, including 38 SECA awards totaling $18.7 million and 110 Core awards totaling $128.0 million.

The following graph shows the total amount of FA funds requested and awarded since FY 2005. The CDFI Program has consistently received more applications than it can fund. In FY 2013, the CDFI Fund capped awards at $1.347 million in an attempt to meet the heavy demand. By capping award amounts, the CDFI Fund was able to make more awards.

CDFI Financial Assistance: Amounts Requested and Awarded
($millions)

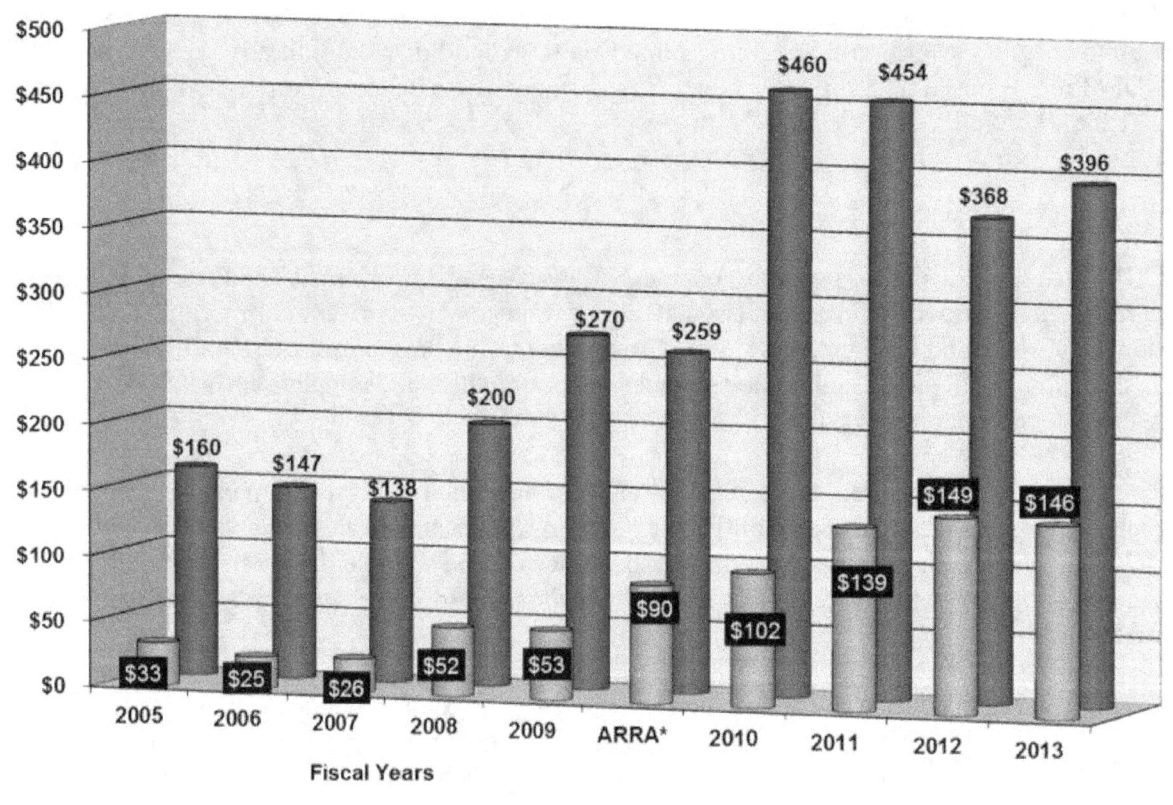

*In February 2009, the CDFI Program received $90 million in funds through the American Recovery and Reinvestment Act (ARRA) to enhance the lending capacity of CDFIs.

14

Healthy Food Financing Initiative

In FY 2011, the CDFI Fund launched the new Healthy Food Financing Initiative (HFFI) in coordination with efforts being undertaken by the U.S. Department of Agriculture (USDA) and the U.S. Department of Health and Human Services (HHS), and provided FA awards through the CDFI Program to support the initiative. The HFFI represents the Federal government's first coordinated step to eliminate "food deserts" – low-income urban and rural areas in the United States with limited access to affordable and nutritious food – by promoting a wide range of interventions that expand the supply of and demand for nutritious foods, including increasing the distribution of agricultural products; developing and equipping grocery stores; and strengthening producer-to-consumer relationships. In addition, the HFFI is part of a larger effort to create quality jobs and promote comprehensive community development strategies to revitalize distressed neighborhoods into healthy and vibrant communities of opportunity. FA awards made through the HFFI can be used to make loans and investments and to provide development services that promote and increase access to healthy food options in low-income communities.

In FY 2013, the CDFI Fund announced more than $22.3 million in FA awards through the CDFI Program to 10 organizations to finance healthy food activities. These CDFIs will use the funds to enhance their capacity to make investments in a range of healthy food projects serving food deserts, including grocery stores, mobile food retailers, farmers markets, cooperatives, corner stores, bodegas, and stores that sell other food and non-food items along with a full range of healthy foods. The awardees were located in 10 states: California, Colorado, Illinois, Kentucky, Massachusetts, North Carolina, New York, Pennsylvania, Texas, and Virginia.

Technical Assistance

Through the Technical Assistance (TA) component of the CDFI Program, the CDFI Fund provides grants to build the capacity of both start-up and existing CDFIs. TA grant funds can be used for items such as staff salaries, benefits, staff training, professional services, supplies, and equipment. Applicants often request funds to analyze their target markets, develop lending policies and procedures, or to build staff lending capacity. There is no matching requirement for applicants seeking TA.

More established CDFIs also use TA grants to build their capacity to provide new products, serve current target markets in new ways, or enhance the efficiency of their operations with upgraded computer hardware and software.

FY 2013 TA Awards

In FY 2013, the CDFI Fund received applications requesting a total of more than $8.1 million in TA-only grants. Forty-three organizations received awards totaling $3.6 million. The following graph shows the total amount of TA awards since 2003.

Total Amount of TA Awards
($millions)

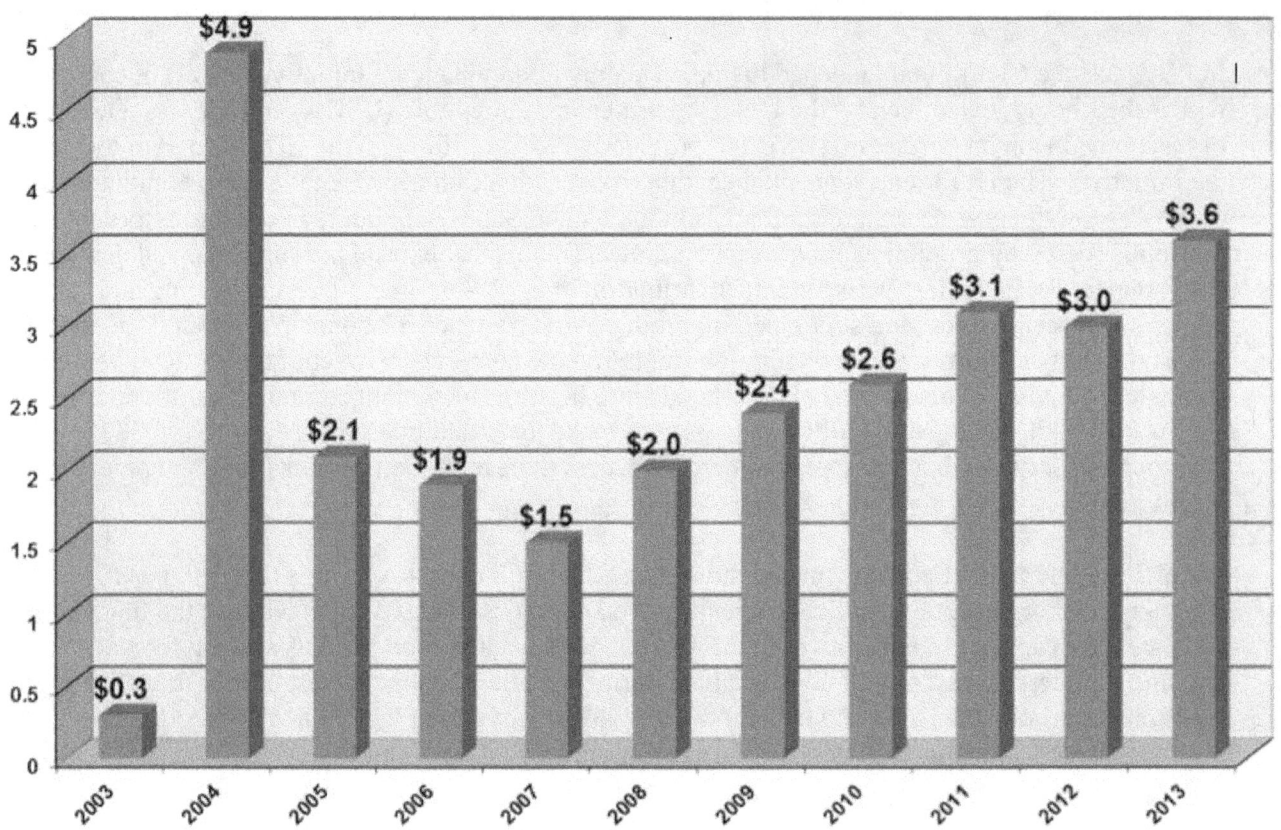

CDFI Program Performance

CDFI Program awardees report their annual performance to the CDFI Fund through the CDFI Fund's Web-based reporting system, the Community Investment Impact System (CIIS). Each awardee has 180 days from its fiscal year end to report through CIIS. This time allows the awardee to complete its annual audit and enables the CDFI Fund to verify reported information against the audit.

The FY 2013 performance information provided here pertains to each awardee's performance results for program year 2012. Please note that the lag in performance reporting reflects the time it takes to deploy funds and make investments for which actual and projected results can be estimated. The delay in performance reporting reflects the length of time from notice of award to award disbursement, the time it takes for an awardee to deploy the funds, and the additional time it takes to compute and report awardee impact information to the CDFI Fund's CIIS reporting system. The FY 2013 performance results reported in the table below reflect program outcomes and activities for 2012 and are based on information entered into CIIS by reporting CDFI Program awardees.

In FY 2013, CDFI awardees reported originating 24,285 loans or investments totaling over $1.9 billion, based on their portfolio of activities in 2012. This includes $484.8 million for 7,112 home improvement and purchase loans, $484.2 million for 8,173 business and microenterprise loans, and $452.8 million for 1,029 residential real estate transactions. These data on the amount and number of loans or investments originated provide baselines for benchmarking and targeting program performance in the forthcoming fiscal year. CDFI Program awardees helped provide funds for projects that created or maintained 35,097 jobs. In addition, real estate loans financed 17,732 affordable housing units, including 15,648 rental units and 2,084 owner units. CDFIs also provided financial products and services to "unbanked" and underserved individuals by maintaining 10,100 Individual Development Accounts totaling $7 million in savings. CDFIs reported providing financial literacy counseling and other training opportunities to 293,666 individuals. Finally, loans and investments originated by CDFIs over the last three years were located in more than 25 percent of eligible census tracts.

Annual Performance of CDFI Program Awardees for FY2013
(Based on Program Activities Reported in 2012)

	Amount
Lending and Investing Activity	
Amount of Total Loans/Investments Originated	**$1,978,165,784**
Number of Total Loans/Investments Originated	24,285
Business and Microenterprise Originations	**$484,245,473**
Number of Originations	8,173
Consumer Originations[1]	**$45,342,740**
Number of Originations	6,583
Home Improvement and Home Purchase Originations	**$484,838,792**
Number of Originations	7,112
Residential Real Estate Originations	**$452,842,614**
Number of Originations	1,029
Commercial Real Estate Originations	**$278,930,277**
Number of Originations	353
All Other Originations	**$231,965,888**
Number of Originations	1,035
Jobs at End of Reporting Period	**35,097**
Affordable Housing Units Financed	**17,732**
Rental Units	15,648
Owner Units	2,084
Business Financed[2]	**6,558**
Percent of Eligible Areas Served[3]	**25.3%**
Financial Access and Literacy	
Open Individual Development Accounts	10,100
Dollars Saved in Individual Development Accounts	$7,117,905
Individuals Served by Financial Literacy or Other Training	293,666

---

[1] Due to changes in reporting requirements during FY2012, not all institutions reported consumer loan originations for this year. The actual value of consumer originations is likely to be higher.
[2] This number reflects netting out businesses that received more than one loan
[3] Defined as the percentage of all eligible Census tracts receiving at least one origination in the past *three* calendar years.

Native Initiatives

The Native Initiatives program was created to increase opportunities for Native American, Alaska Native and Native Hawaiian communities (Native Communities) to access credit, capital, and financial services by creating or expanding CDFIs primarily serving those communities. The Native Initiatives has two main components: the Native American CDFI Assistance Program (NACA Program) and specialized training opportunities available under the CDFI Fund's Capacity Building Initiative.

The program was established after the CDFI Fund published the "Native American Lending Study" in November 2001, which evaluated access to credit, capital, and financial services in Native Communities. The Study affirmed the importance of developing Native CDFIs to play a key role in the broader effort to lead Native Communities into the nation's economic mainstream. Congress subsequently specified that the CDFI Fund use certain amounts of its annual appropriations to facilitate the development of Native CDFIs.

A Native CDFI is a CDFI that is created to primarily serve the needs of Native Communities. As of September 30, 2013, there were 63 certified Native CDFIs.

Native CDFIs focus, largely, on two different financial sectors: 1) affordable housing (housing development and homeownership); and 2) economic development (job creation, business development, and commercial real estate development). Some Native CDFIs serve as national or regional intermediaries, providing financial products and services to local Native CDFIs and other community development organizations.

NACA Program FY 2013

Through the Native American CDFI Assistance (NACA) Program, the CDFI Fund provides two types of funding: 1) Financial Assistance (FA) awards which are only available to certified Native CDFIs; and 2) Technical Assistance (TA) grants, which are available to certified Native CDFIs, Emerging Native CDFIs, and Sponsoring Entities.

FA awards are primarily used as financing capital. FA awards are made in the form of loans, grants, deposits, and equity investments to support the certified Native CDFIs' financing activities, and require the Native CDFI to match the CDFI Fund's award dollar-for-dollar with funds from a non-Federal source. TA grants are generally used to acquire products or services including computer technology, staff training, and professional services, such as market analysis, and support for other general capacity-building activities. TA grants do not have a matching funds requirement. NACA awardees use their awards to increase their capacity to serve their target market and/or to create/become certified CDFIs.

The performance results reported by NACA Program awardees in FY 2013 show Native CDFIs originated 1,508 loans or investments totaling $23.2 million based on their portfolio of activities in 2012.

In FY 2013, the CDFI Fund received 59 NACA eligible applications requesting a total of $24.3 million for both FA and TA funding. The CDFI Fund awarded 35 organizations a total of $12.4 million for both FA and TA funding in FY 2013.

FY 2013 NACA FA Awards

In FY 2013, the CDFI Fund awarded 18 organizations totaling approximately $10.0 million in FA. FY 2013 NACA FA awardees include 16 loan funds and two credit unions. The CDFI Fund capped the FA awards in FY 2013 at $750,000. As a result, the CDFI Fund was able to make more FA awards. The CDFI Fund assumes that the demand will remain high as an increasing number of Native CDFIs put into practice the CDFI Fund's training and continue to build their lending programs.

Technical Assistance Grants

Through the NACA Program, the CDFI Fund provides TA grants, which are available to certified CDFIs, Emerging Native CDFIs, and Sponsoring Entities. Unique to the NACA Program, Sponsoring Entities (typically a Tribe or Tribal entity) create and support fledgling Native organizations as they move toward certification.

FY 2013 NACA TA Awards

In FY 2013, 17 organizations received TA awards totaling $2.4 million. Out of 17 organizations receiving a NACA Program TA award, 14 were loan funds, one was a credit union and two were sponsoring entities. Below is a chart of the NACA TA use of funds categories.

FY 2013 NACA Technical Assistance Uses of Funds Categories

Category	Amount	Percent of Total
Personnel (Salary)	$1,441,844	60.9%
Personnel (Fringe Benefits)	$356,446	15.1%
Training	$87,260	3.7%
Travel	$129,046	5.4%
Professional Services	$321,557	13.6%
Equipment & Other Capital Expenditures	$31,862	1.3%
Total	$2,368,015	100%

Training Initiatives

Through the Native Initiatives, the CDFI Fund engaged a contractor to provide the resources for Native CDFI leaders to identify and address critical challenges of their organization. Please see *The Leadership Journey: Native CDFI Growth and Excellence* in the Capacity Building section for more information.

Capacity Building Initiative

The Capacity Building Initiative is the CDFI Fund's primary means of developing and growing the nation's CDFI industry. Through the Capacity Building Initiative, both certified CDFIs and emerging CDFIs nationwide are eligible to access targeted training and technical assistance. Industry-wide training targets key issues currently affecting CDFIs and the communities they serve, including affordable housing and business lending, portfolio management, risk assessment, foreclosure prevention, general business operations, and liquidity and capitalization challenges. Training is offered at locations where CDFIs work, and technical assistance is often provided on-site. Capacity building plans are designed around the specific needs of participating CDFIs. All CDFIs are able to take advantage of online resource banks hosted on the CDFI Fund website.

Specific training series launched or ongoing in FY 2013 include:

- The *Leadership Journey: Native CDFI Growth and Excellence* series, provided by NeighborWorks® America. This series supports the continued growth and long-term sustainability of experienced Native CDFIs by providing the forum, tools, and resources for Native CDFI leaders to identify and address the critical challenges of their organizations. Since inception, 57 participants attended The Leadership Journey training events, 84 participated in webinars, and 16 CDFIs received technical assistance.

- The *Innovations in Small Business Lending* series, provided by Deloitte Financial Advisory Services LLP. The series supports business-oriented CDFIs that are experienced in providing loans and services to small and medium-sized enterprises. Participants have access to training and customized technical assistance designed to increase services to small businesses and explore new market opportunities. Since inception, 100 participants attended the Innovations in Small Business lending training events, 175 participated in webinars, and 8 CDFIs received technical assistance.

- The *Scaling Up Microfinance* series, provided by Opportunity Finance Network. The series expands the capacity of CDFIs that specialize in microfinance through an advanced training and technical assistance program focused on decreasing costs, building human capital, and improving business models in order to attract investments. Since inception, 88 participants attended the Scaling Up Microfinance lending training events, 454 participated in webinars, and 39 CDFIs received technical assistance.

- The *Strengthening Small and Emerging CDFI* series, provided by Opportunity Finance Network. The series expands the capacity of small and emerging CDFIs through a comprehensive training and technical assistance program. Since inception, 48 participants attended the Strengthening Small and Emerging CDFI training events and 45 CDFIs received technical assistance.

- The *Financing Community Health Centers* series, provided by Opportunity Finance Network. The series will provide advanced training and technical assistance, including one-on-one assistance, and an advanced forum for peer learning for CDFIs to establish and improve services that are critical to the needs of community health centers in an evolving environment. The first training took place in October 2013.

- The *Preserving and Expanding CDFI Minority Depository Institutions* series, provided by Deloitte Financial Advisory Services LLP. The series will address the unique challenges facing CDFI Minority Depository Institutions by providing advanced training and technical assistance. The first training is scheduled to take place in December 2013.

New Markets Tax Credit Program

The New Markets Tax Credit Program (NMTC Program) stimulates capital investment in low-income communities nationwide. The program permits taxpayers to receive a credit against Federal income taxes for making Qualified Equity Investments (QEIs) in designated Community Development Entities (CDEs). Substantially all of QEI proceeds must in turn be used by the CDE to provide investments in low-income communities.

The CDFI Fund is responsible for awarding NMTC allocation authority to CDEs. It does so through a competitive award process. This process ensures that the most qualified organizations receive first consideration for this limited resource.

The NMTC provided to the investor totals 39 percent of the amount of the investment made in a CDE and is claimed over a seven-year credit allowance period. In each of the first three years, the investor receives a tax credit equal to five percent of the total amount paid for the stock or capital interest at the time of purchase. For the final four years, the value of the tax credit is six percent annually. Investors may not redeem their investments prior to the conclusion of the seven-year period.

The NMTC Program was authorized under the Community Renewal Tax Relief Act of 2000. The statute included $15 billion in allocation authority for seven years. Since the NMTC Program was enacted, it has been reauthorized four times; most recently, the Taxpayer Relief Act of 2012 extended the program through 2013. Additionally, the Hurricane Katrina Gulf Opportunity (GO) Zone Act of 2005 authorized an additional $1 billion in allocation authority toward the rebuilding and renewal of the GO Zone, and the American Recovery and Reinvestment Act (Recovery Act) provided an additional $3 billion in allocation authority to assist in the economic recovery. Combined, Congress has authorized the CDFI Fund to award $36.5 billion in NMTC authority through FY 2012.

Additionally, the Tax Relief and Health Care Act of 2006 required that Treasury prescribe regulations to ensure that non-metropolitan counties receive a proportional allocation of QEIs. The CDFI Fund's process for ensuring proportional non-metropolitan investment is described in the NMTC Program calendar year (CY) 2013/2014 Notice of Allocation Availability (NOAA).

Results of the First Ten NMTC Allocation Rounds

NMTC authority allocations are awarded annually through a competitive process. CY 2002 was the first year in which applications for NMTC authority were submitted to the CDFI Fund. To date, the CDFI Fund has completed ten allocation rounds and has made 749 awards totaling $36.5 billion in allocation authority. This amount includes the $3 billion of Recovery Act-authorized allocations ($1.5 billion through the 2008 NMTC allocation round and $1.5 billion through the 2009 NMTC allocation round).

Applications

Round	Number	Amount (Billions)
1	345	$25.8
2	271	$30.4
3	208	$22.9
4	254	$28.3
5	258	$27.9
6	239	$21.3
7	249	$22.5
8	250	$23.5
9	314	$26.7
10	282	$21.9
Totals	**2,670**	**$251.2**

Allocations

Round	Number	Amount (Billions)
1	66	$2.5
2	63	$3.5
3	41	$2.0
4	63	$4.1
5	61	$3.9
6	102	$5.0
7	99	$5.0
8	99	$3.5
9	70	$3.5[1]
10	85	$3.5
Totals	**749**	**$36.5**

Demand for NMTC allocation authority has been high since the program's inception, as 2,670 applicants have requested tax credits supporting a total of more than $251 billion in equity investments – approximately seven times the amount of allocation authority available for awards by the CDFI Fund. Through the first ten allocation rounds, only about 28 percent of applicants were selected to receive an

---

[1] The Tax Relief, Unemployment Insurance Reauthorization and Job Creation Act of 2010 provided $3.5 billion in allocation authority for the CY 2011 Round. In addition to the $3.5 billion, the NMTC Program allocated $122.9 million of unused, rescinded or surrendered allocation authority from prior rounds.

award. The average tax credit allocation award through the first ten rounds was approximately $48.7 million.

CY 2012 NMTC Allocation Round

In April 2013, the CDFI Fund announced that 85 applicants were awarded $3.5 billion in the CY 2012 NMTC allocation round. The 85 applicants selected to receive awards are headquartered in 28 different states and the District Columbia.

These 85 allocatees have committed to achieving results above and beyond minimal program requirements:

All 85 allocatees indicated that 100 percent of their investment dollars would be made either in the form of equity, equity equivalent financing, or debt that is at least 50 percent below market and/or is characterized by at least five concessionary features. Such features include, among other things, subordinated debt, reduced origination fees, higher than standard loan-to-value ratios, lower than standard debt service coverage ratios, non-traditional collateral, and longer than standard amortization periods.

All 85 allocatees committed to providing at least 75 percent of their investments to areas of higher economic distress (and/or areas targeted for development by other government programs) than are minimally required under the NMTC Program.

NMTC Program regulations require that at least 85 percent of QEI dollars be invested into Qualified Low-Income Community Investments (QLICIs). All 85 of the allocatees indicated that they would invest at least 95 percent of QEI dollars into QLICIs. In real dollars, this means that at least $452 million above and beyond what is minimally required by the NMTC Program will be invested into low-income communities.

As detailed in the CY 2012 NOAA, the CDFI Fund sought to ensure that: (1) an appropriate proportion of awards were provided to "Rural CDEs"; and (2) that at least 20 percent of all dollars invested by allocatees under the CY 2012 allocation round are invested in non-metropolitan counties. With respect to the first objective, seven allocatees, receiving allocations totaling $420 million, met the criteria for "Rural CDE" designation. In total, 38 of the 85 allocatees are required to deploy some or all of their investments in non-metropolitan counties. This ensures that approximately $691 million will be deployed in non-metropolitan counties after removing costs for CDE administrative expenses.

CY 2013/CY 2014 NMTC Allocation Round

In CY 2013, the CDFI Fund began the application review process for the 2013/ 2014 NMTC allocation round. The CDFI Fund combined the CY 2013 and CY 2014 rounds in order to achieve cost and efficiency savings to the government in addition to realigning the program calendar. The combined round will also prevent an anticipated deficit of available NMTCs and allow the CDFI Fund to make additional allocation awards. Applications for the CY 2013/2014 NMTC allocation round were due on September 18, 2013. The CDFI Fund received 310 applications for the 2013/2014 NMTC allocation round. The applications requested a total of more than $25.8 billion in NMTC allocation authority.

NMTC Evaluation Research

In 2008, the CDFI Fund contracted with The Urban Institute to conduct the first formal, independent evaluation of the NMTC Program. The evaluation was program-wide in its scope, focusing on program design, execution, outputs, and outcomes. The objective was to provide policymakers with information needed to assess the program's performance; give program administrators and participants useful information for improving the program; and inform and educate the general public with respect to what the NMTC Program is, how it works, and what it accomplishes. Information collection was limited to projects that were initiated during the first four allocation rounds, from 2002 through 2006. The evaluation was based largely on original data collected through three surveys which were based on a random sample of projects. The sample was stratified by project type, award round, investment size, and geography to assure that the sample was representative and large enough to support statistically valid findings.

The overall finding was that in the period studied, the NMTC Program operated as intended — encouraging investments in low-income areas for a diverse range of community and economic development projects, with varying results. The most prevalent results were provision of advantageous financing, real estate development in low-income areas, additions to local tax bases, and job creation or retention. NMTC financed projects also added to or expanded community amenities, services, and facilities and supported small businesses and organizations.

NMTC Activities to Date

Allocation agreements have been executed with each of the 749 allocatees from the first ten rounds. As of September 30, 2013, allocatees had reported raising QEIs totaling more than $31.9 billion. This figure represents almost 87 percent of the $36.5 billion in allocation authority issued to CDEs to date. In fiscal year 2013, over $3.0 billion in QEIs were raised.

Allocatees report QEI and QLICI activity to the CDFI Fund through the Allocation Tracking System (ATS) and Community Investment Impact System (CIIS). Allocatees that have raised QEIs are required to report these investments within 60 days via ATS. Within six months of the end of their fiscal year end, CDEs must complete an annual Institution Level Report (ILR) via CIIS. Allocatees that have made QLICIs are also required to submit an annual Transaction Level Report (TLR) in CIIS. An allocatee's ILR, TLR, and audited financial statements are due 180 days after the end of its fiscal year.

All results in the chart below represent the allocatees' CIIS data reported for fiscal year 2013 (program year 2012). As shown in the table below, for this program year allocatees reported making $4.8 billion of loans and investments in Qualified Active Low Income Community Businesses (QALICBs). In FY 2013, allocatees reported that these funds will create 14,897 jobs and funded construction-related jobs totaling 46,538. In FY 2013, 45.4 percent of the dollars invested were invested in "real estate QALICBs" (i.e., businesses that develop or lease real property for use by others). In addition, 54.0 percent of the dollars were invested in "non-real estate QALICBs" (i.e., operating businesses) in low-income communities, and the remaining investments were direct investments into other CDEs. Allocatees reported providing $892,700 in financial counseling and other services to 3,107 businesses in low-income communities. Adding together all QLICIs yields a grand total of $31.1 billion of cumulative investments was reported in CIIS since 2003.

Annual Performance of NMTC Program Allocatees for FY 2013
(Based on Program Activities Reported in 2012)

	Amount
Lending and Investing Activity	
Total Qualified Low-Income Community Investments (QLICIs)	**$4,839,736,034**
Number of QLICIs	1,207
Real Estate Activity (Investments in QALICBs[1])	**$2,200,063,832**
Number of QLICIs	545
Non-Real Estate Activity (Investments in QALICBs)	**$2,616,686,335**
Number of QLICIs	655
Loans/Investments Made to Other Community Development Entities (CDEs)	**$22,985,867**
Number of QLICIs	7
Percent of Loans/Investments in Severely Distressed Communities[2]	**78.54%**
Jobs at Reporting Period End	**14,897**
Projected Construction Jobs	**46,538**
Affordable Housing Units Financed	**1,856**
Rental Units	570
Owner Units	1,286
Square Feet of Commercial Real Estate	**14,405,247**
Manufacturing	3,179,674
Office	6,893,527
Retail	4,332,046
Businesses Financed	**491**
Financial Counseling and Other Services	
Total Investments	$892,700
Number of Businesses Served	3,107

[1] Qualified Active Low-Income Community Businesses
[2] "Severely distressed" communities include Census tracts with poverty rates above 30 percent; or median family incomes below 60 percent of the metropolitan or state median; or unemployment rates greater than 1.5 times the national average.

Cumulative Performance of NMTC Program Allocatees[1]
(Based on Program Activities Reported in 2003-2012)

	Amount
Lending and Investing Activity	
Total Qualified Low-Income Community Investments (QLICIs)	**$31,137,443,421**
Number of QLICIs	8,063
Real Estate Activity (Investments in QALICBs)	**$17,221,643,392**
Number of QLICIs	3,951
Non-Real Estate Activity (Investments in QALICBs)	**$13,200,144,032**
Number of QLICIs	3,913
Loans/Investments Made to Other Community Development Entities (CDEs)	**$715,655,997**
Number of QLICIs	199
Percent of Loans/Investments in Severely Distressed Communities	**74.15%**
Jobs at Reporting Period End	**207,550**
Projected Construction Jobs	**354,323**
Affordable Housing Units Financed	**11,730**
Rental Units	6,104
Owner Units	5,626
Square Feet of Commercial Real Estate	**149,183,269**
Manufacturing	22,048,876
Office	71,872,637
Retail	55,261,756
Businesses Financed[2]	**4,706**
Financial Counseling and Other Services	
Total Investments	$29,559,584
Number of Businesses Served	32,873

Bank Enterprise Award Program

The Bank Enterprise Award Program (BEA Program) recognizes the key role played by traditional financial institutions in community development lending, investing, and service-related activities. Through the BEA Program, the CDFI Fund provides monetary awards to regulated banks and thrifts for increasing their lending, investments, and service-related activities in economically distressed communities (those with high poverty and unemployment) and/or financial assistance to CDFIs through grants, stock purchases, loans, deposits, and other forms of financial and technical assistance. The size of the award is a percentage of the increase in activities from one annual reporting period to the next.

---

[1] Numbers of Qualified Low-Income Community Investments (QLICIs) refer to the number of transactions, not the number of New Markets Tax Credit projects.
[2] The cumulative estimate of businesses financed nets out those businesses that have reported in multiple years as part of the same project.

26

Providing monetary awards for reinvestment in distressed communities leverages the CDFI Fund's dollars and puts more capital to work in distressed communities throughout the nation. The BEA Program is highly targeted to areas with larger populations. Under the 2000 census data, the BEA program eligibility criteria determined that there are 2,651 fully qualified and 12,020 partially qualified census tracts as distressed communities. Under the five-year American Community Survey census data for 2006-2010, the BEA program eligibility criteria determined that there are 2,167 census tracts that fully qualify and 17,014 census tracts that partially qualify as distressed communities.

BEA Program awards are based on the increase in the amount of Qualified Activities from a Baseline Period to a later Assessment Period (the corresponding time in the following year). Qualified Activities consist of financial or technical assistance provided to certified CDFIs, loans made by financial institutions in distressed communities (for example, affordable housing loans, small business loans, real estate development loans, and education loans), and financial services provided in distressed communities (such as access to automated teller machines, providing financial education workshops and opening of savings accounts).

Promoting CDFI Investments through the BEA Program

The BEA Program prioritizes three types of activities. The first priority is to increase banks' financial support of CDFIs in order to build CDFI self-sufficiency and capacity (referred to as CDFI-Related Activities). The second and third priorities are to build the capacity of FDIC-insured depository institutions to expand their community development lending and investments in severely underserved areas (referred to as Distressed Community Financing Activities and Service Activities, respectively).

The CDFI Fund makes awards to applicants in the CDFI-Related Activities category before making awards to applicants in the Distressed Community Financing Activities category and Service Activities category. The prospect of a BEA Program award encourages banks to achieve this first priority by providing low-cost capital and operating support to CDFIs, which has helped to create and sustain a network of CDFIs. CDFIs serve as conduits for banks to effectively serve highly distressed neighborhoods.

Eligibility

All FDIC-insured depository institutions are eligible to apply for a BEA Program award. As stated above, the BEA Program rewards actual increases in the dollar volume of Qualified Activities from a Baseline Period to a later Assessment Period. Qualified Activities for each of the three main types of bank activities include:

1) CDFI-Related Activities: Equity investments (grants, stock purchases, purchases of partnership interests, limited liability company membership interests, or equity-like loans); and CDFI support activities (loans, deposits or technical assistance) to certified CDFIs (referred to as CDFI Partners).

2) Distressed Community Financing Activities: Loans or investments for affordable home mortgages, affordable housing development, education, home improvement, small businesses,

and commercial real estate development in economically distressed communities.

3) Service Activities: Deposits, financial services (such as check-cashing, money orders, or certified checks), targeted retail savings/investment products (such as electronic transfer accounts - ETAs), targeted financial services (such as individual development accounts - IDAs), or community services provided to low- to moderate-income individuals or the institutions serving them (such as financial education seminars).

FY 2012 BEA Program Awards

The CDFI Fund announced the FY 2012 BEA awardees during the first quarter of FY 2013. Fifty-nine FDIC-insured institutions were selected to receive approximately $18 million in FY 2012 BEA Program awards. In the FY 2012 funding round, awardees provided $603.5 million in qualified loans or investments in distressed communities, $21.6 million in qualified loans, deposits and technical assistance to CDFIs, and $7.3 million in qualified financial services in distressed communities.

FY 2013 BEA Program Awards

In FY 2013, the CDFI Fund received 98 eligible applications requesting a total of approximately $91 million, compared to 71 applications requesting a total of approximately $88.5 million in FY 2012. FY 2013 applicants are headquartered in 27 states and the District of Columbia, compared to the 22 states and the District of Columbia represented in the prior year. In FY 2012, Congress mandated that at least ten percent of the CDFI Fund's appropriations be directed to counties that meet the criteria for Persistent Poverty County1 (PPC) designation. This PPC requirement continued under the current Continuing Resolution for FY 2013 and applicants were required to indicate a minimum and maximum percentage of their award that they would commit to deploying in PPCs.

FY 2013 BEA Community Impact

FY 2013 BEA Program applicants increased their qualified community development activities by $493.5 million over the prior year's awardees:

- $427.8 million increase in loans and investments in distressed communities;

- $55.4 million increase in loans, deposits, and technical assistance to CDFIs; and

- $10.3 million increase in the provision of financial services in distressed communities.

The trend of investments in CDFIs and investments and services in distressed communities by prior year BEA awardees is shown in the Distribution of BEA Program Awards by Category chart below.

---

[1] The appropriation language defined Persistent Poverty Counties as any county that has had 20 percent or more of its population living in poverty over the last 30 years, as measured by the 1990 and 2000 decennial censuses, and the 2010 American Community Survey.

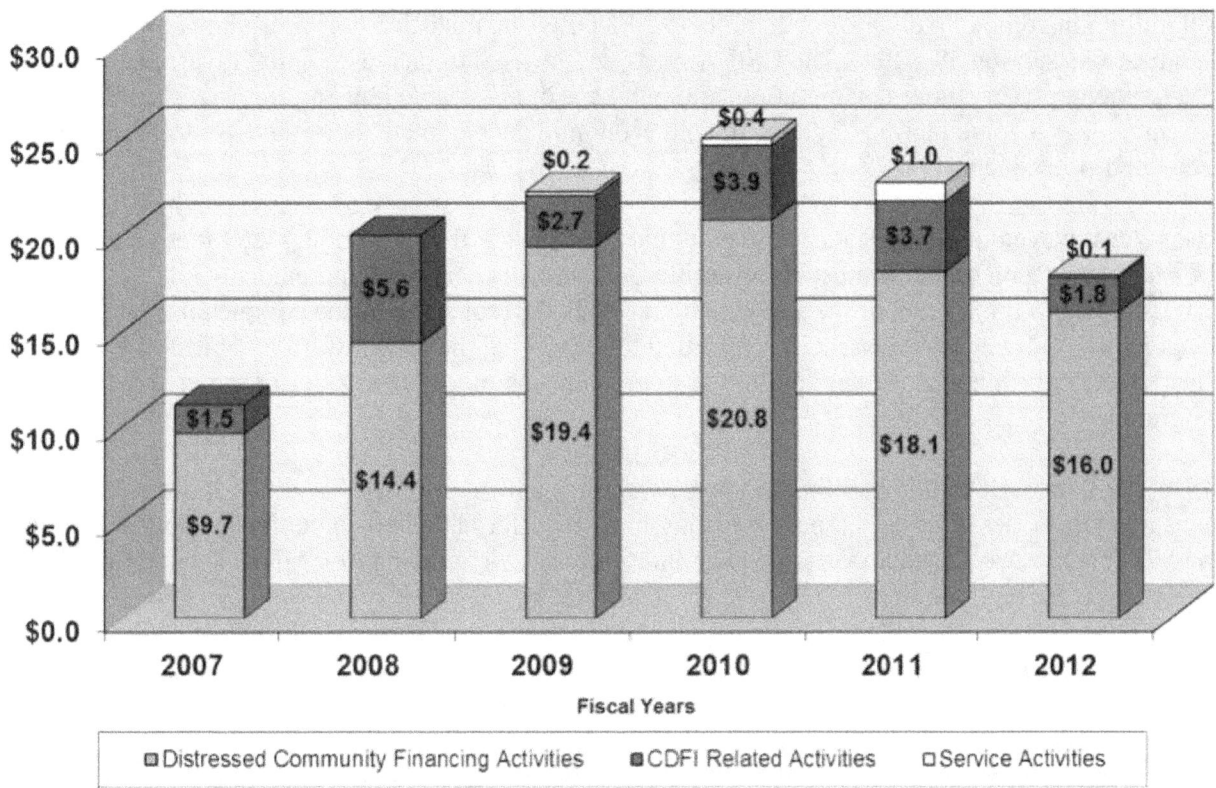

**Distribution of BEA Program Awards
by Category ($millions)**

Fiscal Years

□ Distressed Community Financing Activities　■ CDFI Related Activities　□ Service Activities

Financial Education and Counseling Pilot Program

The program goals of the Financial Education and Counseling Pilot Program (FEC Pilot Program) are to identify successful methods resulting in positive behavioral change for financial empowerment, and to establish program models for organizations to carry out effective financial education and counseling services to prospective homebuyers.

In FY 2010, the CDFI Fund was appropriated $4.1 million for the FEC Pilot Program, of which $3.1 million was specifically appropriated for an award to an organization located in the State of Hawaii and $1 million was appropriated in FY 2010 for the FEC Pilot Program. The CDFI Fund released the NOFA for this program on May 28, 2010, and made award determinations in the first quarter of FY 2011. FY 2010 awardees are located in Florida, Hawaii, New Mexico, and Pennsylvania. No FEC Pilot Program funding has been appropriated since FY 2010.

All awardees are required to submit impact and performance reports for three calendar years following the receipt of grant funds. In CY 2012, awardees exceeded the collective goal of serving 2,360 prospective homebuyers by over 100 percent (5,561), an increase of nearly 2,500 from CY 2011.

Capital Magnet Fund

In its inaugural FY 2010 funding round for the Capital Magnet Fund (CMF), the CDFI Fund announced $80 million in competitively awarded grants to 23 CDFIs and qualified non-profit housing organizations serving 38 states. The CMF awards will be used to increase capital investment for the development, preservation, rehabilitation, and purchase of affordable housing for low-, very low-, and extremely low-income families, and for related economic development activities. No CMF funding has been appropriated since FY 2010.

Awardees received their Assistance Agreement in July 2011 and grant funding later that year. Per the Assistance Agreement, funds must be committed within two years of the agreement (July 2013) and disbursed within three years of the agreement (July 2014). Projects must be completed within 5 years of agreement (July 2016). Awardees committed to leveraging the CMF award by at least 10 times with other sources of capital as well as committed to projects that meet percentages of targeted incomes and geographies.

In FY 2013, the CDFI Fund baselined awardees' performance reporting. For the first two years of CMF investment activities, awardees report investing in 6,301 affordable housing units developed for renters and 502 for affordable home ownership. The interim project leveraging of CMF funds to total eligible project costs are reported to as 11.9.

CDFI Bond Guarantee Program

The CDFI Bond Guarantee Program was enacted through the Small Business Jobs Act of 2010. Through the program, the Secretary of the Treasury will provide a 100 percent guarantee of bonds (including principal, interest, and call premiums) issued by Qualified Issuers. Bonds issued through the program will support CDFI lending and investment activity in underserved communities by providing a source of long-term capital. Qualified Issuers will use bond proceeds to finance loans for eligible community and economic development purposes. In FY 2012, the CDFI Fund developed the program structure and terms and conditions. In FY 2013, the CDFI Fund issued the program's interim regulations, the inaugural Notice of Guarantee Availability (NOGA), and application materials. By the end of FY 2013, funding for three guarantees was obligated in the total amount of $325 million. Subject to Congressional authorization, the CDFI Fund anticipates providing up to $1 billion in guarantees in FY 2014.

Status of Financial Management

This section includes the assurance statement required under the Federal Managers' Financial Integrity Act, a summary of the results of the FY 2013 financial statement audit, a summary of the financial management initiatives of the CDFI Fund during FY 2013, and a discussion of the CDFI Fund's financial position and results of operations during the past fiscal year.

Management Assurances

The Director, Community Development Financial Institutions (CDFI) Fund, is responsible for establishing and maintaining effective internal control over financial reporting and has made a conscientious effort to meet the internal control requirements of the Federal Managers' Financial Integrity Act (FMFIA), the Federal Financial Management Improvement Act (FFMIA), Office of Management and Budget (OMB) Circular A-123, and the Reports Consolidation Act of 2000. The CDFI Fund is operating in accordance with the procedures and standards prescribed by the Comptroller General and OMB guidelines.

The systems of management control for the CDFI Fund organizations under my purview are designed to ensure that:

(a) Programs achieve their intended results;
(b) Resources are used consistent with overall mission;
(c) Programs and resources are free from waste, fraud, and mismanagement;
(d) Laws and regulations are followed;
(e) Controls are sufficient to minimize any improper or erroneous payments;
(f) Performance information is reliable;
(g) System security is in substantial compliance with all relevant requirements;
(h) Continuity of operations planning in critical areas is sufficient to reduce risk to reasonable levels; and
(i) Financial management systems are in compliance with federal financial systems standards, i.e., FMFIA Section 4 and FFMIA.

For all CDFI Fund responsibilities, we provide herein reasonable assurance that the above listed management control objectives, taken as a whole were achieved by our office during FY 2013. Specifically, this assurance is provided with reference to Sections 2 and 4 of the FMFIA. I further assure that the CDFI Fund's financial management systems are in substantial compliance with requirements imposed by FFMIA.

The analytical basis for this assurance being provided is based on management knowledge derived from day-to-day management operations, monitoring of program results, and ongoing observations of staff and program operations.

My assurance is based on the CDFI Fund's assessment of management and internal controls, including existing policies and procedures, knowledge gained from daily management activities, the review of various management information reports attendant to those activities, reports and reviews by internal and external auditors, our annual review performed pursuant to the Improper Payments Information Act, and our own understanding of the requirements imposed by both FMFIA and FFMIA.

Donna J. Gambrell

Director, CDFI Fund

Description of the CDFI Fund's Financial Management System

The CDFI Fund contracts for accounting services through a franchise agreement with the Bureau of Fiscal Service (BFS) in Parkersburg, West Virginia. While the BFS maintains the accounting system relating to the CDFI Fund's transactions, the CDFI Fund is responsible for the generation of all source documents and the accuracy of all accounting information.

The CDFI Fund's financial management system includes the disbursement transactions maintained by BFS in the accounting system, as well as records maintained and procedures performed by the CDFI Fund's financial management staff in the Office of the Deputy Chief Financial Officer (DCFO). The CDFI Fund's resource manager and Treasury's DCFO are responsible for the administrative control of its funds, budget formulation and execution, and review and analysis of financial information.

Results of FY 2013 Financial Statement Audit

The FY 2013 audit of the CDFI Fund's financial statements resulted in an unmodified opinion.

FY 2013 Financial Management Initiatives

In FY 2013, financial management focus was on continuing to implement the information technology initiatives identified in FY 2012.

Community Investment Impact System (CIIS)

CIIS is a Web-based system designed to collect an Institution Level Report (ILR) and Transaction Level Report (TLR) from CDFIs and CDEs. The CIIS data collected from CDFIs include each organization's profile, financial position, portfolio, community impacts, development services, other products and services, and compliance measures. The CIIS data collected from CDEs include each organization's profile, QEI distribution, portfolio, loan purchases, and financial counseling and other services.

Cumulatively through FY 2013, CIIS was used by 690 CDFIs and 278 CDEs to report institutional-level data, with 46 organizations reporting in both categories. Through FY 2013, cumulatively 336 organizations submitted data on more than 571,860 transactions in CDFI loan/investment portfolios.

In July 2013, the CDFI Fund released a report and transactional and project level data on the New Markets Tax Credits (NMTC) program for the 2002-2011 reporting years. The report details how $26.4 Billion in Tax Credits have been invested in revitalizing Low-Income Communities throughout the nation. NMTCs were utilized in over 2,600 businesses and 3,990 real estate investments across the country. NMTCs have been invested in every state and in both urban and rural communities—18.6 percent of the investments have been made in non-metropolitan areas—leading to new growth for areas of the country that have been lagging in the economic recovery. Of the Qualified Low-Income Community Investments (QLICIs) made, the cumulative distribution is as follows:

- 3,990 (58.6 percent of total) QLICIs totaling $17,675,329,192 (66.9 percent of total), were made in real estate development and leasing activities.

- 2,637 (38.7 percent of total) QLICIs totaling $8,037,605,335 (30.4 percent of total) were made in operating businesses.
- 185 (2.7 percent of total) QLICIs t totaling $717,598,673 (2.7 percent of total) were investments in other CDEs.

To maintain its practice of agency transparency, the CDFI Fund released a breakdown of all NMTC investments reported to the CDFI Fund through fiscal year (FY) 2011. The data release is available for use by academics, researchers, and the general public.

In order to comply with the Privacy Act, any personal information identifying borrowers as well as their race, gender, etc. has been suppressed. In addition, in order to ensure the anonymity of borrowers and investors all location information has been limited to city, state, five-digit zip code, and Census tract. Additional safeguards are also in place.

Use of Grants.gov for Paperless Processing of Grant Applications

The Federal Financial Assistance Management Improvement Act (FFAMIA) requires all federal grant-making agencies to migrate 100 percent of their electronic grant program applications to the Grants.gov system administered by the Department of Health and Human Services. In FY 2013, the CDFI Fund achieved 99 percent compliance with the FFAMIA. The CDFI Fund was not able to receive five award applications through Grants.gov (out of 559 total applications). Due to applicant registration delays with the System for Award Management (SAM), five CDFI Fund award applicants were unable to complete the registration process for SAM prior to the application deadline; therefore, these five applicants were unable to use Grants.gov to apply. The CDFI Fund intends to continue working with Grants.gov for the receipt of all future award applications.

Migration to an Award Management Information System for Internal Application Processing

The FFAMIA requires that Federal grant-making agencies migrate their electronic grant processing systems to one of three federally selected Centers of Excellence (CoE). This initiative is known as the "Grants Management Line of Business" (GMLoB).

In July 2010, the CDFI Fund requested a waiver from compliance with GMLoB requirements. The Office of Management and Budget (OMB) approved the request, noting that the CDFI Fund's fit-gap analysis demonstrated that none of the approved consortia aligned well with the CDFI Fund's business processes. OMB also approved the CDFI Fund's request to acquire a new commercial off-the-shelf product to replace its legacy business systems. This product, the Award Management Information System (AMIS), will be an enterprise business system to meet the CDFI Fund's award and tax credit allocation management requirements.

The CDFI Fund is in the acquisition phase for AMIS. Previously, the CDFI Fund had analyzed its mission-oriented business processes and developed a single, enterprise business model that streamlined and eliminated redundancies, and removed stove-piped and program-specific procedures. Based on this enterprise business model, the CDFI Fund developed and released an acquisition package for AMIS. The CDFI Fund plans to award an AMIS contract in the second quarter of FY 2014 and complete deployment of AMIS in FY 2016. With the deployment of AMIS, the CDFI Fund expects to be able to handle larger volumes of grants, tax credits, and loan portfolios while achieving more transparency and better data quality, and providing better service to customers.

Federal Funding Accountability and Transparency Act

Effective October 2010, the Federal Funding Accountability and Transparency Act of 2006 (FFATA) and its 2008 amendments require that all Federal grant-making agencies report on their grant activities on a publicly viewable website, USASpending.gov. This creates a new obligation for awardees under the CDFI Fund's award programs to maintain active accounts in the System for Award Management (SAM), to identify their locations, the places where most of their activities are concentrated, provide information about any first-tier subawards and about the compensation of the five most highly paid people within the organizations (subject to certain thresholds). In order to comply with this requirement, the CDFI Fund includes the standard award terms as stipulated by FFATA in its assistance agreements and monitors the data quality of the information provided to the USASpending.gov through the Federal Assistance Award Database System Plus. In addition, the CDFI Fund has developed complementary guidance and highlights FFATA reporting requirements during post-award web-seminars for all of the grant programs at the CDFI Fund to include the CDFI Program, the NACA Program, the FEC Pilot Program, the CMF, and other programs that Congress may authorize and appropriate for the CDFI Fund to administer.

Improper Payments Elimination and Recovery Act of 2010 (IPERA)

On July 22, 2010, President Obama signed into law the Improper Payments Elimination and Recovery Act (IPERA, Pub. L. 111-204). Office of Management and Budget (OMB) implementing guidance Memorandum M-11-04, Increasing Efforts to Recapture Improper Payments by Intensifying and Expanding Payment Recapture Audits, dated November 16, 2010, states that bureaus are responsible for increasing efforts to recapture improper payments by intensifying and expanding Payment Recapture Audits under IPERA. The CDFI Fund is working with the Bureau of Fiscal Service and Departmental Offices in order to prevent and recapture improper payments.

Management Responsibilities

CDFI Fund management is responsible for the fair presentation of information contained in the principal financial statements in conformity with accounting principles generally accepted in the United States of America. Management is also responsible for the fair presentation of the CDFI Fund's performance measures in accordance with the Office of Management and Budget requirements. The quality of the CDFI Fund's internal control structure rests with management, as does the responsibility for identification of and compliance with applicable laws and regulations.

Limitations of the Financial Statements

The financial statements report the financial position and results of operations of the CDFI Fund for the fiscal year ending on September 30, 2013, pursuant to the requirements of 31 U.S.C. 3515(b). While the statements have been prepared from the books and records of the CDFI Fund in conformity with accounting principles generally accepted in the United States of America, the statements are in addition to the financial reports used to monitor and control budgetary resources which are prepared from the same books and records. The statements should be read with the realization that they are for a component of the U.S. Government, a sovereign entity, and that the payment of all liabilities other than for contracts can be abrogated by the sovereign entity.

Analysis of Financial Position and Results of Operations

Summarized Financial Data
(Amounts in Millions)

	FY 2013	FY 2012	Increase / (Decrease)
Assets	$297.3	$283.7	$13.6
Liabilities	$41.4	$58.2	($16.8)
Net Position	$255.9	$225.6	$30.3
Revenue and Financing Sources	$181.6	$172.3	$9.3
Expenses	$180.7	$172.9	$7.8
Excess (Shortage) of Revenue and Financing			
Net Gain (Net Loss)	$0.9	($0.6)	$1.5

Allocation of Fund Assets
September 30, 2013
(Amounts in Millions)

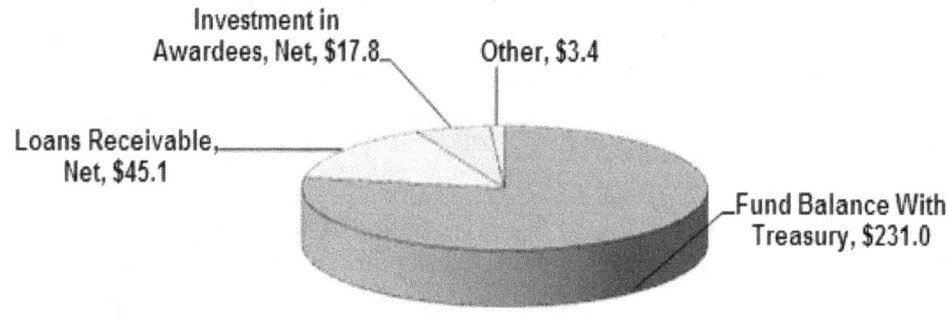

Investment in Awardees, Net, $17.8

Other, $3.4

Loans Receivable, Net, $45.1

Fund Balance With Treasury, $231.0

☐ Fund Balance With Treasury   ☐ Loans Receivable, Net   ☐ Investment in Awardees, Net   ☐ Other

Assets

Assets increased by $13.6 million during FY 2013, consisting primarily of a $7.3 million increase in the Fund Balance with Treasury which includes appropriated and borrowed funds available to pay liabilities and to finance authorized award and purchase commitments. Loans receivable also increased $7.0 million due to new loans issued in FY13.

Fund Balance with Treasury
The Fund Balance with Treasury reflected a $7.3 million increase from the prior year, due to differences in the timing of when appropriation revenue is received versus when expenses are paid.

Loans Receivable
Loans receivable are increased when loan awards (under the CDFI and NACA programs) are disbursed by the CDFI Fund and decreased for loan repayments and loan write-offs. During FY 2013, net loans increased by $7.0 million resulting, in part, from new loans of $14.2 million and loan repayments of $4.6 million.

Investments
The CDFI Fund currently holds four types of investments with net balances as follows:

- Non-voting equity securities - $13.6 million
- Convertible subordinated debt - $0.5 million
- Limited partnerships - $1.7 million
- Secondary Capital - $2.1 million

The primary source of financial data used for the majority of assessments is the most recent audited financial statements of the investees. These assessments determine whether any other–than–temporary impairments should be recognized.

Liabilities

The decrease in liabilities during the year of $16.8 million consisted primarily of a decrease in awards payable of $22.2 million. This was partially offset by an increase in debt of $4.5 million.

Awards Payable
Awards payable consists primarily of CDFI Program awards of $0.5 million. Awards payable decreased by $22.2 million in FY 2013 as the conditions for payment for the 2013 CDFI Program awards were not met during FY2013 thus these awards are classified as commitments rather than payables.

Debt
During FY 2013, the CDFI Fund borrowed $8.5 million for new loans, $0.9 million due to a downward subsidy reestimate and $0.4 million to meet annual interest payments due to the Treasury Department, at interest rates ranging from 1.78% to 6.48%, depending on maturity dates or risk categories. The CDFI Fund borrowing was partly offset by the repayments of amounts borrowed from Treasury totaling $5.3 million. Principal repayments collected from awardee loans during the year are used to repay the

Treasury borrowings, and therefore amounts collected and repaid to Treasury each year will vary from year to year, as they are a function of awardee loan terms.

Net Position

Net position increased during the year by $30.3 million. Net position will change during the year as a result of the following: 1) the difference between appropriations received (net of appropriations cancelled, rescinded and adjusted for credit subsidy reestimates) and appropriations used; 2) any adjustment of the CDFI Fund's subsidy reestimate; and 3) the excess (shortage) of revenue and financing sources over (under) expenses. During FY 2013, appropriations received and appropriations for subsidy reestimate (net of amounts cancelled, rescinded and downward subsidy reestimate) were $208.9 million, and appropriated capital used was $179.5 million resulting in an increase in net position of $29.4 million. This increase in net position was further increased by the $0.9 million gain recorded by the CDFI Fund in FY 2013.

Revenue and Financing Sources

The primary source of revenue and financing sources for the CDFI Fund is the annual appropriation used to fund expenses ("appropriated capital used" as reflected in the statement of operations). Pursuant to Federal grant accounting requirements, the amount of appropriated funds recognized as revenue is, with certain adjustments, equal to the amount of operating expenses for the year. Operating expenses for the year, excluding those paid by others, were $178.2 million.

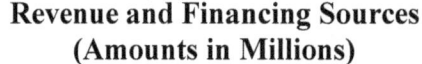

Revenue and Financing Sources
(Amounts in Millions)

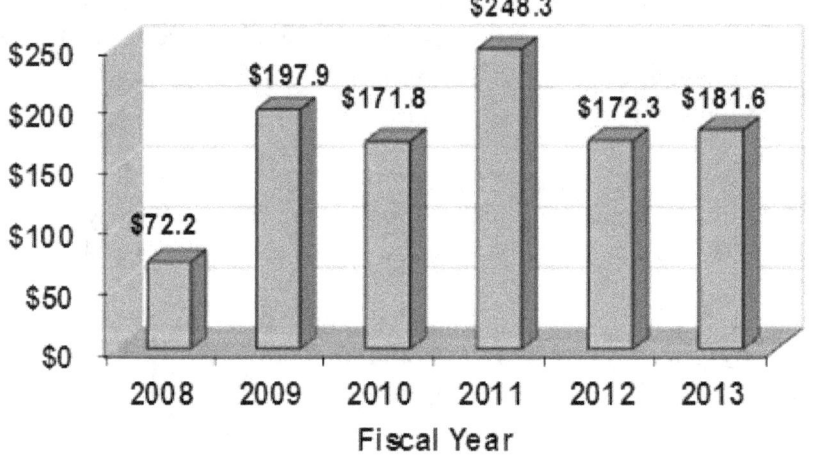

Expenses

The change in the CDFI Fund's operating expenses, excluding administrative expenses paid by others during FY 2013 consisted of the following:

Comparison of Operating Expenses Excluding Administrative Expenses Paid by Others
Fiscal Years 2013 and 2012
(Amounts in Millions)

	FY 2013	FY 2012	Difference
Award Expenses	$148.1	$148.6	($0.5)
Administrative Expenses	$27.6	$20.6	$7.0
Bad Debt Expense	$2.5	$0.8	$1.7
Total Operating Expenses	$178.2	$170.0	$8.2

Award Expenses
Award expenses during the year decreased $0.5 million. CDFI Program award expenses increased $3.4 million and BEA award expenses decreased $3.9 million due to the timing of the awards.

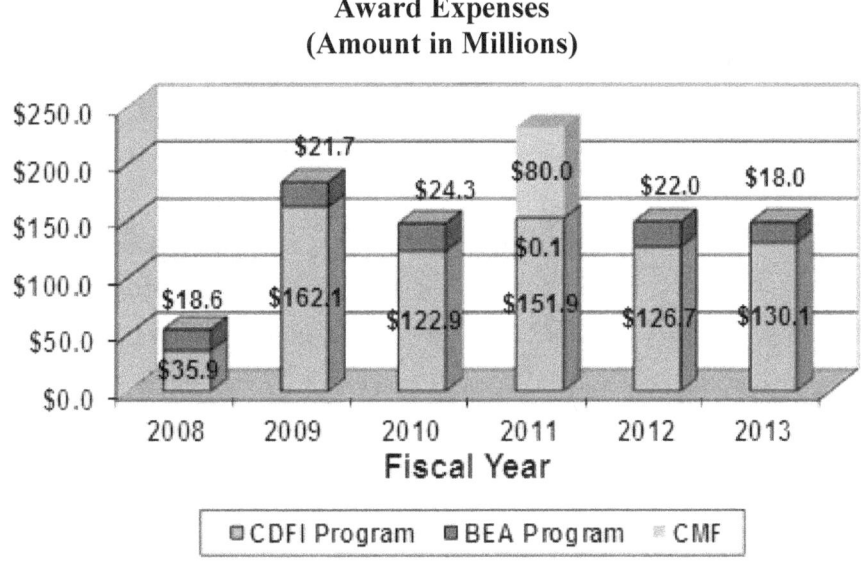

Administrative Expenses
Administrative expenses increased by $7.0 million during FY 2013 due to $4.0 million in Bond Guarantee Program expenses, that were previously appropriated to a Bond Guarantee Program administrative account that expired at the end of FY12 and a $2.8 million increase in contractual services resulting from information technology enhancement projects.

Bad Debt Expense
Bad debt expense is a function of the impairment related to loans receivable at year-end including impact of certain loan modifications made during the year. The CDFI Fund performs an analysis process that includes an individual review of certain loans using key financial ratios from the awardees' most recent audited financial statements. The remainder of the loans are collectively evaluated for impairment. Bad debt expense increased during FY 2013 by $1.7 million due to an increase in delinquent and impaired loans.

Net Gain

As stated above, the amount of appropriated capital used (the largest component of the CDFI Fund's revenue) is, with certain adjustments, equal to the amount of operating expenses for the year. Accordingly, the excess of revenue and other financing sources over expenses (net gain) will consist of the amount by which revenue and financial sources other than appropriated capital used exceeds expenses not covered by budgetary resources.

For FY 2013, expenses not covered by budgetary resources totaled $1.7 million, consisting of interest expense on Treasury borrowings. Interest and dividend income totaled $1.2 million.

KPMG LLP
Suite 12000
1801 K Street, NW
Washington, DC 20006

Independent Auditors' Report

Inspector General
U.S. Department of the Treasury

Director
Community Development Financial Institutions Fund

Report on the Financial Statements

We have audited the accompanying financial statements of the U.S. Department of the Treasury's Community Development Financial Institutions Fund (CDFI Fund), which comprise the statements of financial position as of September 30, 2013 and 2012, and the related statements of operations and changes in net position, and cash flows for the years then ended, and the related notes to the financial statements.

Management's Responsibility for the Financial Statements

Management is responsible for the preparation and fair presentation of these financial statements in accordance with U.S. generally accepted accounting principles; this includes the design, implementation, and maintenance of internal control relevant to the preparation and fair presentation of financial statements that are free from material misstatement, whether due to fraud or error.

Auditors' Responsibility

Our responsibility is to express an opinion on these financial statements based on our audits. We conducted our audits in accordance with auditing standards generally accepted in the United States of America; the standards applicable to financial audits contained in *Government Auditing Standards* issued by the Comptroller General of the United States; and Office of Management and Budget (OMB) Bulletin No. 14-02, *Audit Requirements for Federal Financial Statements*. Those standards and OMB Bulletin No. 14-02 require that we plan and perform the audit to obtain reasonable assurance about whether the financial statements are free from material misstatement.

An audit involves performing procedures to obtain audit evidence about the amounts and disclosures in the financial statements. The procedures selected depend on the auditors' judgment, including the assessment of the risks of material misstatement of the financial statements, whether due to fraud or error. In making those risk assessments, the auditor considers internal control relevant to the entity's preparation and fair presentation of the financial statements in order to design audit procedures that are appropriate in the circumstances, but not for the purpose of expressing an opinion on the effectiveness of the entity's internal control. Accordingly, we express no such opinion. An audit also includes evaluating the appropriateness of accounting policies used and the reasonableness of significant accounting estimates made by management, as well as evaluating the overall presentation of the financial statements.

We believe that the audit evidence we have obtained is sufficient and appropriate to provide a basis for our audit opinion.

Opinion on the Financial Statements

In our opinion, the financial statements referred to above present fairly, in all material respects, the financial position of the U.S. Department of the Treasury's Community Development Financial Institutions Fund as of September 30, 2013 and 2012, and the results of its operations and its cash flows for the years then ended in accordance with U.S. generally accepted accounting principles.

Other Matters

Other Information

Our audits were conducted for the purpose of forming an opinion on the basic financial statements as a whole. The information in the Community Development Financial Institutions Fund Overview, Program Discussion and Analysis, and Status of Financial Management sections is presented for purposes of additional analysis and is not a required part of the basic financial statements. Such information has not been subjected to the auditing procedures applied in the audits of the basic financial statements, and accordingly, we do not express an opinion or provide any assurance on it.

Other Reporting Required by *Government Auditing Standards*

In accordance with *Government Auditing Standards*, we have also issued our report dated December 12, 2013 on our consideration of the CDFI Fund's internal control over financial reporting and our report dated December 12, 2013 on our tests of its compliance with certain provisions of laws, regulations, contracts, and grant agreements and other matters. The purpose of those reports is to describe the scope of our testing of internal control over financial reporting and compliance and the results of that testing, and not to provide an opinion on the internal control over financial reporting or on compliance. Those reports are an integral part of an audit performed in accordance with *Government Auditing Standards* in considering the CDFI Fund's internal control over financial reporting and compliance.

KPMG LLP

December 12, 2013

KPMG LLP
Suite 12000
1801 K Street, NW
Washington, DC 20006

Independent Auditors' Report on Internal Control Over Financial Reporting

Inspector General
U.S. Department of the Treasury

Director
Community Development Financial Institutions Fund

We have audited, in accordance with auditing standards generally accepted in the United States of America; the standards applicable to financial audits contained in *Government Auditing Standards* issued by the Comptroller General of the United States; and Office of Management and Budget (OMB) Bulletin No. 14-02, *Audit Requirements for Federal Financial Statements*, the financial statements of U.S. Department of the Treasury's Community Development Financial Institutions Fund (CDFI Fund), which comprise the statements of financial position as of September 30, 2013 and 2012, and the related statements of operation and changes in net position, and cash flows for the years then ended, and the related notes to the financial statements, and have issued our report thereon dated December 12, 2013.

Internal Control Over Financial Reporting

In planning and performing our audit of the financial statements as of and for the year ended September 30, 2013, we considered the CDFI Fund's internal control over financial reporting (internal control) to determine the audit procedures that are appropriate in the circumstances for the purpose of expressing our opinion on the financial statements, but not for the purpose of expressing an opinion on the effectiveness of the CDFI Fund's internal control. Accordingly, we do not express an opinion on the effectiveness of the CDFI Fund's internal control. We did not test all internal controls relevant to operating objectives as broadly defined by the *Federal Managers' Financial Integrity Act of 1982*.

A deficiency in internal control exists when the design or operation of a control does not allow management or employees, in the normal course of performing their assigned functions, to prevent, or detect and correct, misstatements on a timely basis. A material weakness is a deficiency, or a combination of deficiencies, in internal control, such that there is a reasonable possibility that a material misstatement of the entity's financial statements will not be prevented, or detected and corrected on a timely basis. A significant deficiency is a deficiency, or a combination of deficiencies, in internal control that is less severe than a material weakness, yet important enough to merit attention by those charged with governance.

Our consideration of internal control was for the limited purpose described in the first paragraph of this section and was not designed to identify all deficiencies in internal control that might be material weaknesses or significant deficiencies. Given these limitations, during our audit we did not identify any deficiencies in internal control that we consider to be material weaknesses. However, material weaknesses may exist that have not been identified.

Purpose of this Report

The purpose of this report is solely to describe the scope of our testing of internal control and the result of that testing, and not to provide an opinion on the effectiveness of the CDFI Fund's internal control. This report is an integral part of an audit performed in accordance with *Government Auditing Standards* in considering the CDFI Fund's internal control. Accordingly, this communication is not suitable for any other purpose.

KPMG LLP

December 12, 2013

KPMG LLP
Suite 12000
1801 K Street, NW
Washington, DC 20006

Independent Auditors' Report on Compliance and Other Matters

Inspector General
U.S. Department of the Treasury

Director
Community Development Financial Institutions Fund

We have audited, in accordance with auditing standards generally accepted in the United States of America; the standards applicable to financial audits contained in *Government Auditing Standards* issued by the Comptroller General of the United States; and Office of Management and Budget (OMB) Bulletin No. 14-02, *Audit Requirements for Federal Financial Statements*, the financial statements of U.S. Department of the Treasury's Community Development Financial Institutions Fund (CDFI Fund), which comprise the statements of financial position as of September 30, 2013 and 2012, and the related statements of operations and changes in net position, and cash flows for the years then ended, and the related notes to the financial statements, and have issued our report thereon dated December 12, 2013.

Compliance and Other Matters

As part of obtaining reasonable assurance about whether the CDFI Fund's financial statements are free from material misstatement, we performed tests of its compliance with certain provisions of laws, regulations, contracts, and grant agreements, noncompliance with which could have a direct and material effect on the determination of financial statement amounts, and certain provisions of other laws and regulations specified in OMB Bulletin No. 14-02. However, providing an opinion on compliance with those provisions was not an objective of our audit, and accordingly, we do not express such an opinion. The results of our tests of compliance disclosed no instances of noncompliance or other matters that are required to be reported herein under *Government Auditing Standards* or OMB Bulletin No. 14-02.

Purpose of this Report

The purpose of this report is solely to describe the scope of our testing of compliance and the result of that testing, and not to provide an opinion on the CDFI Fund's compliance. This report is an integral part of an audit performed in accordance with *Government Auditing Standards* in considering the CDFI Fund's compliance. Accordingly, this communication is not suitable for any other purpose.

KPMG LLP

December 12, 2013

Financial Statements and Notes

COMMUNITY DEVELOPMENT FINANCIAL INSTITUTIONS FUND

Statements of Financial Position as of September 30, 2013 and 2012

	2013	2012
Assets		
Fund balance with Treasury (Note 5)	$ 231,037,336	223,738,732
Advances and prepayments	258,897	155,920
Loans receivable, net of allowance for bad debts of $9,404,359 in 2013 and $7,822,492 in 2012 (Note 6)	45,073,805	38,119,879
Investments, amortized cost (Note 7)	2,608,290	3,636,860
Investments, cost method (Note 9)	13,554,770	14,554,770
Investments, equity method (Note 10)	1,671,258	2,405,372
Interest and other receivable	1,857,719	491,426
Internal-use software, net of accumulated amortization of $4,617,539 in 2013 and $4,458,544 in 2012	276,016	435,011
Internal-use software in development	956,851	208,345
Total assets	$ **297,294,942**	**283,746,315**
Liabilities and Net Position		
Accounts payable	$ 2,119,430	1,104,506
Awards payable	548,915	22,782,621
Accrued payroll	429,840	541,847
Accrued annual leave	626,673	582,756
Due to the General Fund (Note 11)	24,737	-
Debt (Note 12)	37,650,048	33,180,363
Total liabilities	41,399,643	58,192,093
Commitments (Note 13)		
Unexpended appropriations (Note 14)	238,370,980	208,892,405
Cumulative results of operations	17,524,319	16,661,817
Total net position	**255,895,299**	**225,554,222**
Total liabilities and net position	$ **297,294,942**	**283,746,315**

The accompanying notes are an integral part of these statements.

COMMUNITY DEVELOPMENT FINANCIAL INSTITUTIONS FUND

Statements of Operations and Changes in Net Position
Years Ended September 30, 2013 and 2012

	2013	2012
Revenue and financing sources:		
Appropriations	$ 179,535,267	169,650,386
Imputed other income - expenses paid by others (Note 15)	845,641	903,840
Interest, non-federal	983,038	918,960
Interest, federal	145,676	82,572
Dividends	92,188	131,919
Other	156,573	260,811
Equity in income (loss) of associates, net	(160,208)	352,146
Total revenue and financing sources	181,598,175	172,300,634
Expenses:		
CDFI grants (Note 16)	130,090,223	126,682,863
BEA grants	17,969,543	21,951,000
Administrative expenses (Note 17)	27,611,488	20,580,133
Increase in bad debt expense (Note 6)	2,532,738	769,511
Administrative expenses paid by others (Note 15)	845,641	903,840
Total operating expenses	179,049,633	170,887,347
Interest expense, federal	1,686,040	1,742,070
Impairment losses	-	145,764
Discount on investments	-	169,079
Total expenses	180,735,673	172,944,260
Net income (loss)	$ 862,502	(643,626)
Cumulative results of operations, beginning of year	$ 16,661,817	17,305,443
Net income (loss)	862,502	(643,626)
Cumulative results of operations, end of year	$ 17,524,319	16,661,817

The accompanying notes are an integral part of these statements.

COMMUNITY DEVELOPMENT FINANCIAL INSTITUTIONS FUND

Statements of Cash Flows
Years Ended September 30, 2013 and 2012

		2013	2012
Cash flows from operating activities:			
Net income (loss)	$	862,502	(643,626)
Adjustments to reconcile net income (loss) to net cash used in operations:			
Impairment losses		-	145,764
Discount on investments		-	169,079
Equity in income (loss) of associates		160,208	(352,146)
Amortization expense		158,995	166,586
Accretion of discount		(71,430)	(73,307)
Increase in bad debt expense		2,532,738	769,511
Change in assets and liabilities:			
Decrease (increase) in advances and prepayments		(102,977)	113,075
Increase in interest and other receivable		(1,366,293)	(195,254)
Increase in accounts payable, accrued payroll, and Due to the General Fund		927,654	530,546
Decrease in awards payable		(22,233,706)	(19,970,220)
Increase in accrued annual leave		43,917	72,258
Net cash used in operating activities		(19,088,392)	(19,267,734)
Cash flows from investing activities:			
Proceeds from redemption of investments		2,100,000	100,000
Proceeds from distribution of investments		573,906	561,995
Internal-use software in development		(748,506)	(208,345)
Recovery of loan written off in prior year		49,129	-
Loans disbursed		(14,160,895)	-
Collection of loan principal		4,625,102	6,358,188
Net cash (used in) provided by investing activities		(7,561,264)	6,811,838
Cash flows from financing activities:			
Increase in unexpended appropriations, net		29,478,575	47,955,237
Borrowings from Treasury		9,818,731	4,158,278
Borrowing re-payments to Treasury		(5,349,046)	(6,709,221)
Net cash provided by financing activities		33,948,260	45,404,294
Net change in Fund Balance with Treasury		7,298,604	32,948,398
Fund Balance with Treasury, beginning of year		223,738,732	190,790,334
Fund Balance with Treasury, end of year	$	231,037,336	223,738,732

The accompanying notes are an integral part of these statements.

(1)   Description of Reporting Entity

The Community Development Financial Institutions Fund (CDFI Fund) was created as a bipartisan initiative in the Riegle Community Development and Regulatory Improvement Act of 1994 (Public Law No. 103-325). The CDFI Fund was placed in the Department of the Treasury and began operations in July 1995.

The CDFI Fund operates various programs aimed at expanding the availability of credit, investment capital, and financial and other services in distressed urban, rural, and Native American communities. The CDFI Fund is intended to help create a national network of financial institutions dedicated to community development that leverages private resources (financial and human) to address community development needs.

The major programs operated by the CDFI Fund are the Community Development Financial Institutions Program (consisting of a Financial Assistance and Technical Assistance Component), the New Markets Tax Credit Program, the Bank Enterprise Awards Program, Native Initiatives and the Capital Magnet Fund.

The Community Development Financial Institutions (CDFI) Program provides financial and technical assistance awards to certified community development financial institutions (CDFIs) which in turn provide services to create community development impact in underserved markets. Financial assistance awards take the form of grants, direct loans, and equity investments. Technical Assistance grants provide assistance to start-up and early-stage CDFIs and entities planning to become CDFIs.
The CDFI Fund implemented the New Markets Tax Credit (NMTC) Program during fiscal year 2002. Under this program, the CDFI Fund provides an allocation of tax credits to Community Development Entities (CDEs), which use these credits to attract private sector investment. Proceeds from these investments are used for community development purposes. Unlike the CDFI Fund's grant programs, the allocation of tax credits to CDEs has no effect on the financial statements of the CDFI Fund.

The Bank Enterprise Award (BEA) Program provides incentives to insured depository institutions (banks and thrifts) to invest in CDFIs and to increase their lending and financial services in distressed communities. Program participants are selected based on projected achievements. The awards are disbursed only after the activities have been implemented successfully, to ensure that only completed activities are recognized and that the CDFI Fund's limited dollars are effectively leveraged with private capital.

Through the Native American CDFI Assistance (NACA) Program, a component of the Native Initiatives, the CDFI Fund provides grants to help create CDFIs and to build the capacity of existing Native CDFIs that serve primarily Native American, Alaska Native, and Native Hawaiian communities.

(2)   Community Development Financial Institutions Bond Guarantee Program

The CDFI Bond Guarantee Program was enacted through the Small Business Jobs Act of 2010 (Public Law 111-240) on September 27, 2010. The CDFI Fund will serve as the program administrator and the U.S. Department of the Treasury (Treasury Department) will guarantee the full amount of notes or bonds issued to support CDFIs that make investments for eligible community or economic development purposes. The bonds or notes are intended to support CDFI lending and investment by providing a source of long-term, patient capital to CDFIs. The law provides $13.5 million be made available to the CDFI Fund to establish and administer the program. In fiscal year 2013, the CDFI Fund promulgated program regulations, a notice of guarantee availability, and application materials, thereby commencing program implementation. Funds were obligated for the first guarantees during the fiscal year with disbursements expected to occur in fiscal year 2014.

(3)   Limitations of the Financial Statements

The financial statements report the financial position and results of operations of the CDFI Fund for the fiscal years ending on September 30, 2013 and 2012, pursuant to the requirements of 31 U.S.C. 3515(b). While the statements have been prepared from the books and records of the CDFI Fund in conformity with accounting principles generally accepted in the United States of America, the statements are in addition to the financial reports used to monitor and control budgetary resources which are prepared from the same books and records. The statements should be read with the realization that they are for a component of the U.S. Government, a sovereign entity, and that the payment of all liabilities other than for contracts can be abrogated by the sovereign entity.

(4)   Summary of Significant Accounting Policies

(a)   Basis of Presentation

The American Institute of Certified Public Accountants (AICPA) has designated the Federal Accounting Standards Advisory Board (FASAB) as the standards-setting body for financial statements of federal governmental entities, with respect to the establishment of accounting principles generally accepted in the United States of America. SFFAS 34, issued by FASAB, provides authoritative guidance allowing federal entities to prepare financial statements in conformance with accounting and reporting principles issued by the Financial Accounting Standards Board (FASB). Accordingly, the CDFI Fund financial statements are presented in accordance with accounting standards published by FASB.

(b)   Use of Estimates

The preparation of financial statements in conformity with accounting principles generally accepted in the United States of America requires management to make estimates and assumptions that affect the reported amounts of assets and liabilities and disclosure of contingent assets and liabilities at the date of the financial statements and the reported amounts of revenues and expenses during the reporting period. Actual results could differ from these estimates. Significant items subject to such estimates include allowance for bad debts and the identification and valuation of investment impairments.

(c)   Fund Balance with Treasury

The CDFI Fund does not maintain cash in commercial bank accounts. The Treasury Department processes cash receipts and disbursements. Fund Balance with Treasury is composed primarily of appropriated and borrowed funds (financing and program accounts) that are available to pay liabilities and finance authorized award and purchase commitments.

(d)   Loans Receivable, net of Allowance for Bad Debts

Loans receivable relate to direct loans made to certain CDFI Program awardees and are recorded at face value on the closing date. Direct and incremental loan costs are deemed to be de minimis. Any interest is recognized over the life of the loan, when earned. Amounts collected on loans receivable are included in cash flows from investing activities in the statements of cash flows. During fiscal years 2013 and 2012, the CDFI Fund received requests from awardees requesting an extension of their maturity dates. The requests were processed in collaboration with the Department of the Treasury Office of the Deputy Chief Financial Officer (DCFO). A restructuring of a loan constitutes a troubled debt restructuring for purposes of FASB ASC-310-40 if the creditor grants a concession to the debtor that it would not otherwise consider. While the loan extensions are being processed, awardees do not make principal payments. The CDFI Fund continues to accrue and collect interest on all loans that are under restructuring subject to determination about eventual collectability.

The allowance for bad debts is the CDFI Fund's best estimate of the amount of credit losses in the CDFI Fund's existing loans. The allowance includes both specific and non-specific loan analysis. The non-specific portion of the allowance considers historical loss experience adjusted for current factors. The historical loss experience is based on actual loss history experienced by the CDFI Fund over the most recent seven years. This actual loss experience is supplemented with other economic factors that include consideration of the following: levels of and trends in delinquencies and impaired loans; levels of and trends in write-offs; the number of loan restructurings processed in the current year; and the recent performance of previously restructured loans. The specific portion is determined on an individual basis upon review of any loan that has a past due balance or no payment required until maturity, was modified during the year, or was included in the specific allowance in the prior year. A loan is considered impaired if it is probable that the CDFI Fund will not collect all principal and interest contractually due. The impairment is measured based on the present value of the expected future cash flows discounted at the loan's effective interest rate. Impairment losses are charged against the allowance and increases in the allowance are charged to bad debt expense. Loans are written off against the allowance when all possible means of collection have been exhausted and the potential for recovery is considered remote.

COMMUNITY DEVELOPMENT FINANCIAL INSTITUTIONS FUND
Notes to Financial Statements
September 30, 2013 and 2012

(e) *Interest and Other Receivable*

Interest is accrued on the outstanding loans receivable principal balances and investments based on stated rates of interest as earned and when determined collectible. Interest is not accrued past the maturity date of loans receivable and investments.

(f) *Investments*

The CDFI Fund provides assistance to certain for-profit CDFI program awardees by purchasing various investments described below. The CDFI Fund is restricted from owning more than 50% of the equity of awardees and from controlling their operations. Held-to-maturity debt securities are those debt securities in which the CDFI Fund has the ability and intent to hold the security until maturity. None of the investments meet the criteria for Variable Interest Entity Accounting.

Non-voting Equity Securities: These investments are carried at original cost subject to other-than-temporary impairments.

Secondary Capital Interests: These interests are held-to-maturity and carried at amortized cost, net of applicable discounts, subject to other-than-temporary impairments.

Convertible Subordinated Debt: This instrument exhibits sufficient characteristics of an equity security as the CDFI Fund is entitled to any dividends in the non-voting common stock as if the CDFI Fund had converted the debentures into such stock prior to the declaration of the dividend. This investment is held-to-maturity and carried at amortized cost, net of applicable discounts, subject to other-than-temporary impairments.

Limited Partnership Interests: These interests are carried in accordance with the equity method of accounting by recognizing the pro-rata share of investee profit/loss through the statement of operations. Investments are further subject to assessment of any other-than-temporary impairments as discussed below.

Certificates of Deposits: These investments are held-to-maturity and recognized at cost as they are fully insured.

Held-to-maturity debt securities are recorded at amortized cost, adjusted for the amortization of premiums or discounts. Premiums and discounts are amortized over the life of any related held-to-maturity security as an adjustment to yield using the straight-line method.

For non-voting equity securities and limited partnerships, a decline in the fair value of any security below cost that is deemed to be other-than-temporary results in an impairment to reduce the carrying amount to fair value. The impairment is charged to earnings and a new cost basis for the security is established. To determine if an impairment is other-than-temporary, the CDFI

53

Fund considers whether (1) it has the ability and intent to hold the investment until a market price recovery and (2) evidence indicating the cost of the investment is recoverable outweighs evidence to the contrary. Evidence considered in this assessment includes the reasons for the impairment, the severity and duration of the impairment, changes in value subsequent to year-end, forecasted performance of the investee, and the general market condition in the industry in which the investee operates.

(g)   *Internal-Use Software*

Internal-use software represents the completed phases of various software placed in service pertaining to 1) processing applications – this software automates the award application submission process; 2) geocoding – web-based software that geocodes addresses, census tracts and counties, and enables applicants to determine the funding eligibility of census tracts and counties under CDFI's various programs; and 3) the Community Investment Impact System (CIIS) – a web-based data collection system for CDFI's and Community Development Entities. The software is amortized using the straight-line method over the estimated useful life of seven years. Amortization expense for the years ended September 30, 2013 and 2012 was $158,995 and $166,586, respectively.

(h)   *Internal-Use Software in Development*

Internal-use software encompasses software design, development, and testing of projects adding significant new functionality and long-term benefits. Costs for developing internal-use software are accumulated in internal-use software in development until a project is placed into service, and testing and final acceptance are successfully completed. Once completed the costs are transferred to internal-use software.

(i)   *Leases*

At the beginning of each fiscal year the CDFI Fund obtains the estimated annual amount for all operating leases. The CDFI Fund then establishes an obligation to be recorded within the financial system for the full amount of the estimate. The CDFI Fund approves each monthly Intra-governmental Payment and Collection transaction and submits the approved form to the Bureau of the Fiscal Service (BFS) for processing on a monthly basis. Rent payments are recognized on a straight-line basis over the term of the lease.

(j)   *Awards Payable*

CDFI Program and CMF grant expense is recognized and awards payable are recorded when the CDFI Fund is made aware, in writing, that the awardee has met the conditions required for payment and the CDFI Fund approves a grant disbursement to be made. BEA Program grant expense is recognized and awards payable are recorded when the CDFI Fund approves the BEA award to be made (i.e. at the time the funds are obligated).

(k) Retirement Plans

CDFI Fund employees participate in the Civil Service Retirement System (CSRS) or the Federal Employees' Retirement System (FERS). The FERS was established by the enactment of Public Law 99-335. Pursuant to this law, FERS and Social Security automatically cover most employees hired after December 31, 1983.

Employees hired prior to January 1, 1984, were provided an opportunity to join either FERS and Social Security or remain in CSRS. The amount of cost recognized by the CDFI Fund for these contributions for the years ended September 30, 2013 and 2012 was $799,653 and $764,252, respectively.

For all employees, a Thrift Savings Plan (TSP) account is automatically established, and the employee can have up to a predetermined maximum amount withheld from their base salary, which is deposited into their TSP account. For FERS employees only, the CDFI Fund makes matching contributions ranging from 1% to 4% for employees who contribute to their TSP account (there is no matching contribution for CSRS employees). The amount of cost recognized by the CDFI Fund for these contributions for the years ended September 30, 2013 and 2012 was $307,336 and $276,937, respectively.

In addition, CDFI Fund employees participating in CSRS have 7% of their base salary withheld which is contributed into a Retirement Fund. The CDFI Fund contributes the same amount into the Retirement Fund. The amount of cost recognized by the CDFI Fund for these contributions for the years ended September 30, 2013 and 2012 was $62,422 and $45,686, respectively. FERS employees and CSRS reinstatement employees are eligible to participate in the Social Security program for retirement. In these instances, the CDFI Fund remits the employer's share of the required contribution.

(l) Annual, Sick, and Other Leave

Annual leave and compensatory leave is accrued as a liability when earned by the employee, and the accrual is reduced as leave is taken. The balance in this accrued liability account is computed using current pay rates. Sick leave and other types of non-vested leave are expensed as the leave is taken.

(m) Debt

Debt represents borrowings payable to the Treasury Department that were made to fund direct loans made by the CDFI Program and other aspects of permissible borrowing authority. Principal repayments to the Treasury Department are required to be made based on the collections of loans receivable and are due September 30 of each year of maturity.

(n) Contingencies

Liabilities for loss contingencies arising from claims, assessments, litigation, fines, penalties and other sources are recorded when it is probable that a liability has been incurred and the amount of the obligation can be reasonably estimated. Legal costs incurred in connection with loss contingencies are expensed as incurred. The CDFI Fund currently has no contingent liabilities meeting the disclosure or recognition thresholds.

(o)   *Revenue and Other Income*

The CDFI Fund receives the majority of its funding through appropriations from the U.S. Congress. The CDFI Fund receives two-year appropriations that may be used, within statutory limits, for awards and operating expenses. Appropriations are recognized as revenues at the time the CDFI Fund's grants are recorded as expenses, and when administrative expenses and provision for bad debts covered by budgetary resources are incurred.
Occasionally, the CDFI Fund receives dividends on its equity investments and may use those funds for awards and operating expenses. Dividends are recognized when earned.
Additional revenue is obtained from interest received on direct loans and on uninvested funds held by the Treasury Department. Interest is recognized when earned and determined to be collectible.

(p)   *Tax Status*

The CDFI Fund, as a government entity, is not subject to federal, state, or local income taxes and, accordingly, no provision for income tax is recorded.

(q)   *Fair Value Measurements*

The CDFI Fund applies the provisions of ASC Topic 820, Fair Value Measurements, for fair value measurements of financial assets and financial liabilities and for fair values measurements of nonfinancial items that are recognized or disclosed at fair value in the financial statements on a nonrecurring basis. This standard defines fair value, establishes a consistent framework for measuring fair value and expands disclosure requirements for fair value measurements. This standard establishes a fair value hierarchy that prioritizes the inputs to valuation techniques used to measure fair value. The hierarchy gives the highest priority to unadjusted quoted prices in active markets for identical assets or liabilities (Level 1 measurements) and the lowest priority to measurements involving significant unobservable inputs (Level 3 measurements). The three levels of the fair value hierarchy are as follows:

- Level 1 inputs are quoted prices (unadjusted) in active markets for identical assets or liabilities that the CDFI Fund has the ability to access at the measurement date.

- Level 2 inputs are inputs other than quoted prices included within Level 1 that are observable for the asset or liability, either directly or indirectly.

- Level 3 inputs are unobservable inputs for the asset or liability.

See Note 8 for more information and disclosures relating to the CDFI Fund's fair value measurements.

(r)   Newly Issued Accounting Standards

In April 2011 FASB issued Accounting Standards Update 2011-02, A Creditor's Determination of Whether a Restructuring is a Troubled Debt Restructuring, providing amendments to ASC Topic 310, Receivables.   The objective of these amendments is to clarify the guidance on a creditor's evaluation of whether it has granted a concession and whether a debtor is experiencing financial difficulties for purposes of determining whether a restructuring constitutes a troubled debt restructuring. For nonpublic entities the disclosures are effective for annual reporting periods ending on or after December 15, 2012. There was no material impact on its statements of financial position or statements of operations.

In May 2011, the FASB issued Accounting Standards Update 2011-04, Amendments to Achieve Common Fair Value Measurement and Disclosure Requirements in U.S. GAAP and IFRS, providing amendments to ASC Topic 820, Fair Value Measurements. The new standards do not extend the use of fair value but, rather, provide guidance about how fair value should be applied where it already is required or permitted under IFRS or U.S. GAAP. For U.S. GAAP, most of the changes are clarifications of existing guidance or wording changes to align with IFRS. A nonpublic entity is required to apply the ASU prospectively for annual periods beginning after December 15, 2011. There was no material impact on its statements of financial position or statements of operations.

(5)   Fund Balance with Treasury

Fund Balance with Treasury as of September 30, 2013 and 2012 consisted of the following components:

	2013	2012
Available	$33,044,466	$43,293,027
Obligated	$187,727,236	$176,682,185
Expired	$10,265,634	$3,763,520
Total	**$231,037,336**	**$223,738,732**

Fund Balance with Treasury includes appropriated and borrowed funds available to pay liabilities and to finance authorized award and purchase commitments.

(6)   Loans Receivable

The CDFI Fund assesses and monitors the credit quality of its loans on an ongoing basis using audited financial statements of awardees. All loans receivable are considered part of the CDFI Fund's business loan portfolio; the CDFI Fund does not further disaggregate loans by segment or class. All loans receivable have been assessed and monitored through September 30, 2013.

The CDFI Fund is exposed to several risk factors related to its loans receivable:
Risk of a deteriorating economic climate and its impact on the CDFI Fund's collection of loans. Economic, industry, and geographic risks associated with unsecured loans to small financial institutions.

As of September 30, 2013 the CDFI Fund had a total recorded investment in impaired loans from troubled debt restructurings of $4,182,500 of which $3,782,500 had a related allowance for bad debt of $2,402,500. The amount of the recorded investment in impaired loans for which there is no related allowance for bad debt is $400,000. The CDFI Fund had a total recorded investment in other impaired loans of $736,870 and a $736,870 related allowance for bad debt. As of September 30, 2012 the CDFI Fund had a total recorded investment in impaired loans from troubled debt restructurings of $4,402,500 of which $3,582,500 had a related allowance for bad debt of $2,322,500. The amount of the recorded investment in impaired loans for which there is no related allowance for bad debt is $820,000. The CDFI Fund had a total recorded investment in other impaired loans of $1,636,870 and a $1,546,870 related allowance for bad debt.

During the years ended September 30, 2013 and 2012 the CDFI Fund had average recorded investments in impaired loans of $4,556,870 and $5,766,037, respectively. During these years the CDFI Fund recognized related interest income of $87,978 and $99,950, respectively. The CDFI Fund recognizes interest income on impaired loans as earned in accordance with loan agreements.

For the years ended September 30, 2013 and 2012, grants in the amount of $2,907,612 and $0, respectively, were disbursed to debtors owing receivables whose terms have been modified in troubled debt restructurings. As of September 30, 2013 and 2012 there were commitments in the amount of $4,711,920 and $4,961,418, respectively to disburse grants to debtors owing receivables whose terms have been modified in troubled debt restructurings.

The activity in the allowance for bad debt and recorded investment in loans receivable for the years ended September 30, 2013 and 2012 were as follows:

	2013	2012
Allowance for bad debt:		
Beginning balance	$7,822,492	$7,052,981
Write-offs	(1,000,000)	-
Recoveries	49,129	-
Provision	2,532,738	769,511
	9,404,359	**7,822,492**
Individually evaluated for impairment	3,139,370	3,869,370
Collectively evaluated for impairment	6,264,989	3,953,122
Loans Receivable:		

	2013	2012
Individually evaluated for impairment	7,573,338	9,093,338
Collectively evaluated for impairment	46,904,826	36,849,033
Total	**$54,478,164**	**$45,942,371**

The CDFI Fund utilizes a rating system to classify loans according to credit worthiness and risk. Each loan is categorized as pass, doubtful or loss.

A description of each category (credit quality indicator), in terms of the attributes of the borrower, the business environment in which the borrower operates or the loan itself, follows:

Credit Quality Indicators

Pass: Timely interest and principal payments; strong debt service capacity, liquidity and viability; very favorable operating environment.

Doubtful: Weak debt service capacity, liquidity and/or viability; evidence of financial deterioration; likely to repay but with hardship.

Loss: Poor financial performance; serious liquidity, debt service capacity and/or viability issues; going concern issues; full loss is probable.

The credit quality indicators for loans receivable as of September 31, 2013 and 2012 were as follows:

	2013	2012
Pass	$49,958,794	$40,723,001
Doubtful	$2,300,000	$2,250,000
Loss	$2,219,370	$2,969,370
Total	**$54,478,164**	**$45,942,371**

The following table provides an analysis of the aging of the past due loans receivable as of September 31, 2013 and 2012:

	30-60 Days Past Due	61-90 Days Past Due	Greater than 90 Days Past Due	Total Past Due	Current	Total Financing Receivables	Recorded Investment > 90 Days and Accruing
2013	$ -	-	486,870	486,870	53,991,294	54,478,164	250,000

COMMUNITY DEVELOPMENT FINANCIAL INSTITUTIONS FUND
Notes to Financial Statements
September 30, 2013 and 2012

	30-60 Days Past Due	61-90 Days Past Due	Greater than 90 Days Past Due	Total Past Due	Current	Total Financing Receivables	Recorded Investment > 90 Days and Accruing
2012	$ -	-	1,150,000	1,150,000	44,792,371	45,942,371	-

The following table illustrates certain required information related to impaired loans as of September 31, 2013 and 2012:

2013	Recorded Investment	Unpaid Principal Balance	Related Allowance	Average Recorded Investment	Interest Income Recognized
With no related allowance recorded:					
Loans	$ 400,000	400,000	-	400,000	6,000
With an allowance recorded:					
Loans	4,519,370	4,519,370	3,139,370	4,156,870	81,978
Total	$ 4,919,370	4,919,370	3,139,370	4,556,870	87,978

2012	Recorded Investment	Unpaid Principal Balance	Related Allowance	Average Recorded Investment	Interest Income Recognized
With no related allowance recorded:					
Loans	$ 820,000	820,000	-	546,667	20,600
With an allowance recorded:					
Loans	5,219,370	5,219,370	3,869,370	5,219,370	79,350
Total	$ 6,039,370	6,039,370	3,869,870	5,766,037	99,250

The loans receivable in nonaccrual status as of September 30, 2013 and 2012 are as follows:

	2013	2012
Total	$ 236,870	$ 1,150,000

(7) Investment Securities

The carrying amount, net of applicable discounts, gross unrealized holding losses and fair value of held-to-maturity debt securities by major security type at September 30, 2013 and 2012 are as follows:

	Aggregate Fair Value	Gross Unrealized Loss	Amortized Cost (Net Carrying Amount)
Investments, Held-to-Maturity at September 30, 2013:			
Convertible debt securities	$500,515	-	$500,515
Secondary capital securities	$2,107,775	-	$2,107,775
Total	**$2,608,290**	**-**	**$2,608,290**
Investments, Held-to-Maturity at September 30, 2012:			
Certificates deposit	$50,000	-	$50,000
Convertible debt securities	$456,412	-	$456,412
Secondary capital securities	$3,130,448	-	$3,130,448
Total	**$3,636,860**	**-**	**$3,636,860**

Maturities of debt securities classified as held-to-maturity were as follows at September 30, 2013:

	Fair Value	Net Carrying Amount
Held-to-Maturity:		
Due within one year	-	-
Due after one through five years	$25,002	$25,002
Due after five through ten years	$2,082,773	$2,082,773
Due after ten years	$500,515	$500,515
	$2,608,290	**$2,608,290**

The CDFI Fund evaluates whether unrealized losses on investment securities indicate other-than-temporary impairment. Significant factors considered include investee audit opinions, regulatory findings and trends in various financial criteria. Based on this evaluation, the CDFI Fund recognized no other-than-temporary impairment losses of these investments in 2013 or 2012.

Convertible debt securities consist of non-interest bearing convertible subordinated debentures. As of September 30, 2013 and 2012, this category consists of one debenture of $2 million notional amount (amortized cost of $500,515 and $456,412 as of September 30, 2013 and 2012, respectively) which matures January 2048 with the option to convert into 200,000 shares of non-voting class B common stock at a $10 per share conversion price.

Secondary capital securities consist of investments that cannot be redeemed prior to scheduled redemption dates.

Certificate of deposit is an investment in a federal credit union awardee, and has an interest rate of zero percent.

(8)   Fair Value Measurements

(a)   *Fair Value of Financial Instruments*

The following table presents the carrying amounts and estimated fair values of the CDFI Fund's financial instruments at September 30, 2013 and 2012. The fair value of an instrument is the amount that would be received to sell an asset or paid to transfer a liability in an orderly transaction between market participants at the measurement date.

	2013 Carrying Amount	2013 Fair Value	2012 Carrying Amount	2012 Fair Value
Financial assets:				
Fund Balance with Treasury	$231,037,336	$231,037,000	$223,738,732	$223,739,000
Loans receivable	45,073,805	34,017,000	38,119,879	27,594,000
Investments, amortized cost	2,608,290	2,608,000	3,636,860	3,637,000
Investments, cost method	13,554,770	24,284,000	14,544,770	21,497,000
Interest and other receivable	$1,857,719	$1,858,000	$491,426	$491,000
Financial liabilities:				
Awards payable	548,915	549,000	22,782,621	22,783,000
Debt	37,650,048	26,203,000	33,180,363	21,658,000

The following methods and assumptions were used to estimate the fair value of each class of financial instrument:

Fund Balance with Treasury, interest and other receivable and awards payable: The carrying amounts, at face value or cost plus accrued interest, approximate fair value because of the short maturity of these instruments.

Loans receivable, debt and investments, amortized cost: The fair value is determined as the present value of future contractual cash flows discounted at an interest rate that reflects the risks inherent in those cash flows. The discount rates approximate rates currently offered by local lending institutions for loans of similar terms to companies with comparable risk. The fair value of nonperforming loans is determined as the present value of expected future cash flows discounted at an interest rate that reflects the risks inherent in those cash flows.   The expected cash flows were estimated based on the awardee's financial condition and the long-term potential of the business in relation to the maturity date of the loan. The fair value of certificates of deposit is discounted cash flow at a market rate.

Investments, cost method: The CDFI Fund records these equity investments under the cost method of accounting. The CDFI Fund considers qualitative assessments of the viability of the investee, fundamental financial analysis and evaluation of the financial statements of the investee and prospects for its future.

(b) *Fair Value Hierarchy*

The CDFI Fund does not record investments or loans at fair value on a recurring basis. However, from time-to-time, the CDFI Fund records nonrecurring fair value adjustments to reflect partial write-downs that are based on current financial indicators of the awardees. The CDFI Fund uses qualitative assessments of the viability of the awardee, evaluation of the financial statements of the awardee and prospects for its future. Financial statement disclosures and audit opinions were reviewed for the most recent five years for indications of going concern or operational issues. Calculations of pro-rata equity, financial performance ratios, total cash and other trend analysis were performed to determine fair value.

There were no assets measured at fair value on a nonrecurring basis in 2013 or 2012 that were still on the balance sheet at year end.

(9) Cost Method Investments

Investments accounted for under the cost method consist of non-voting common stock held in for-profit CDFI Program awardees and preferred non-voting stock held in two awardees. The aggregate amount of these investments is $13,554,770 and $14,554,770 at September 30, 2013 and 2012, respectively. All securities were evaluated for impairment. No investments were written off during fiscal year 2013. One investment was written off during fiscal year 2012 totaling $56,000.

(10) Equity Method Investments

Investments accounted for under the equity method consist of a Class B limited partnership interest in Sustainable Jobs Fund, LP (12%), an interest in Pacific Community Ventures (10%) and a non-voting redeemable transferable interest in BCLF Ventures II, LLC (18%). Equity method investments totaled $1,671,258 and $2,405,372 at September 30, 2013 and 2012, respectively.

(11) Due to the General Fund

The General Fund consists of assets and liabilities used to finance the daily and long-term operations of the U.S. Government, as a whole. It also includes accounts used in the management of the Budget of the U.S. Government.

Due to the General Fund represents a liability to reflect assets owed by the CDFI Fund to the General Fund. These liabilities are separately reported on the Balance Sheet, with a corresponding amount reported in Interest and other receivable. As of September 30, 2013, the General Fund liabilities include penalty and late fees due to delinquent loans totaling $24,737; there were no delinquent loans in 2012.

(12) Debt and Other Borrowings

Debt consists of amounts borrowed from the Treasury Department and included the following activity for the years ended September 30, 2013 and 2012:

	2013	**2012**
Beginning balance	$33,180,363	$35,731,306
New borrowings	9,818,731	4,158,278
Repayments	(5,349,046)	(6,709,221)
Ending balance	**$37,650,048**	**$33,180,363**

The payments to the Treasury Department are due on September 30 of each year of maturity. Principal payments on this debt as of September 30, 2013 are as follows:

Fiscal Year	**Principal Payments**
2014	$ -
2015	333,324
2016	-
2017	1,445,630
2018	$1,491,396
Later years, through 2045	34,379,698
	$37,650,048

During fiscal year 2013, the CDFI Fund borrowed $8,459,720 for new loans, $997,230 due to downward subsidy reestimate and $361,781 to meet annual interest payments due to the Treasury Department, at interest rates ranging from 1.78% to 6.48%, depending on maturity dates or risk categories.

During fiscal year 2012, the CDFI Fund borrowed $3,705,275 due to downward subsidy reestimate and $453,003 to meet annual interest payments due to the Treasury Department, at interest rates ranging from 1.85% to 6.48%, depending on maturity dates or risk categories.

Interest paid in cash for the years ended September 30, 2013 and 2012 was $1,685,900 and $1,742,006, respectively.

The CDFI Fund has permanent indefinite borrowing authority to fund downward subsidy reestimates and annual interest payments to the Treasury Department. These costs do not reduce the CDFI Fund's net position.

The CDFI Fund has permanent indefinite borrowing authority of $436,062,500 to fund the Bond Guarantee Program.

(13)   Commitments

(a)   *Operating Leases*

The CDFI Fund leases office space in Washington, D.C. under the terms of an implicit operating lease between the General Services Administration and Eleven Eighteen Limited Partnership which expires in March, 2019. The CDFI Fund also leases equipment under the terms of an operating lease. The total operating lease expense was $932,804 and $931,544 for the years ended September 30, 2013 and 2012, respectively.

Future minimum payments due under these operating leases as of September 30, 2013 were as follows:

Fiscal Year	Minimum Lease Payments
2014	$ 914,218
2015	912,528
2016	912,528
2017	912,528
2018	912,528
	$4,564,330

(b)   *Award, Purchase and Bond Guarantee Program Commitments*

As of September 30, 2013 and 2012, unfilled award commitments amounted to $185,840,022 and $151,664,176, respectively. Award commitments relate to CDFI Program, NACA Program and CMF awards which were approved by CDFI Fund management but not disbursed as of the end of the year. These award commitments are not considered liabilities at year-end because the awardees have not met the conditions required for payment. Award commitments pertaining to the BEA Program of $0 and $208,091 as of September 30, 2013 and 2012, respectively, represent reimbursable expenditures and are excluded from these amounts since they are reflected as liabilities on the CDFI Fund's balance sheet. Award commitments pertaining to CDFI Program of $548,915 and $22,574,530 as of September 30, 2013 and 2012, respectively, are also reflected as liabilities as these awardees have met the conditions required for payment.

Purchase commitments of $7,849,306 and $15,039,755 as of September 30, 2013 and 2012, respectively, relate to the unexpired portion of contracts, and purchase orders relating to goods and services not yet received.

As of September 30, 2013 and 2012, Bond Guarantee Program commitments amounted to $325,000,000 and $0, respectively.

(14) Unexpended Appropriations

Unexpended appropriations for the years ended September 30, 2013 and 2012 were as follows:

	2013	**2012**
Beginning unexpected appropriations	$208,892,405	$160,937,168
Appropriations received	221,000,000	221,000,000
Appropriations for Subsidy Reestimate	853,092	899,248
Appropriations cancelled	(282,394)	(588,350)
Appropriation rescission	(11,559,626)	-
Appropriations expended	(179,535,267)	(169,650,386)
Downward Subsidy Reestimate Adjustment	(997,230)	(3,705,275)
Change in unexpended appropriations	29,478,575	47,955,237
Ending unexpended appropriations	$238,370,980	$208,892,405

(15) Imputed Financing

Imputed financing represents specific expenses relating to the CDFI Fund paid for by another Federal organization. The components of imputed financing include pension costs for CSRS and FERS retirement plans, Health Benefits Program costs, Group Life Insurance Program costs and audit fees. Imputed financing expenses for the years ended September 30, 2013 and 2012 were $845,641 and $903,840, respectively.

(16) CDFI Program Grant Expense

The CDFI Fund had CDFI Program grant expense of $130,090,223 and $126,682,863 as of September 30, 2013 and 2012, respectively.

(17) Administrative Expenses

Administrative expenses consist of the following for the years ended September 30, 2013 and 2012:

	2013	2012
Personnel compensation and benefits	$9,440,198	$8,841,839
Bond Guarantee Program expenses	6,029,946	2,012,987
Travel	46,089	169,547
Rent, communications, utilities and miscellaneous charges	1,083,094	1,172,277
Contractual services with other agencies	5,682,239	3,413,984
Contractual services with external parties	4,982,270	4,443,276
Information technology systems maintenance	16,915	84,691
Amortization	158,995	166,586
Supplies and printing	160,410	213,192
Other	11,332	61,754
Total	**$27,611,488**	**20,580,133**

(18) Related Party Transactions

The CDFI Fund has Interagency agreements with the Treasury Department. As of September 30, 2013 and 2012, these related party expenses amounted to $8,363,591 and $3,726,659, respectively. As of September 30, 2013 and 2012 related party receivables were $258,897 and $274,763, respectively.

Expenses were recorded as follows for fiscal years 2013 and 2012: Interagency Agreements with Departmental Offices (DO) for financial management services, conference and events, postage, human resources services, and Working Capital Fund shared IT servicesfor the amount of $3,891,762 and $1,537,343 for fiscal years 2013 and 2012, respectively. An Interagency Agreement with the BFS for accounting services, e-Travel and Prism for the amount of $1,077,810 and $953,125 for fiscal years 2013 and 2012, respectively. An Interagency Agreement with Alcohol and Tobacco Tax and Trade Bureau for IT services for the amount of $3,295,196 and $1,236,191 for fiscal years 2013 and 2012, respectively. An Interagency Agreement with Office of Financial Stability (OFS) for personnel for the amount of $98,823 and $0 for fiscal years 2013 and 2012, respectively.

Receivables were recorded as follows as of September 30, 2013 and 2012: Interagency receivables with DO for IT shared services for $258,897 and $274,763, respectively.

(19) Subsequent Events

The CDFI Fund has evaluated subsequent events from the date of statements of financial position through December 12, 2013, the date at which the financial statements were available to be issued, and determined there are no other items to disclose.

Appendix A: Glossary of Acronyms

A
AFR – Agency Financial Report
AMIS – Award Management Information System
ARC – Administrative Resource Center
ARRA – American Reinvestment and Recovery Act of 2009
ATS – Allocation Tracking System

B
BEA – Bank Enterprise Award

C
CCME – Certification, Compliance Monitoring and Evaluation
CDCI – Community Development Capital Initiative
CDE – Community Development Entity
CDFI – Community Development Financial Institution
CDFI Fund – Community Development Financial Institutions Fund
CIIS – Community Investment Impact System
CMF – Capital Magnet Fund
CoE – Centers of Excellence
COTS – Commercial Off-The-Shelf

E
ETA – Electronic Transfer Accounts

F
FA – Financial Assistance
FDIC – Federal Deposit Insurance Corporation
FEC – Financial Education and Counseling Pilot Program
FFAMIA – Federal Financial Assistance Management Improvement Act
FFATA – Federal Funding Accountability and Transparency Act
FFMIA – Federal Financial Management Improvement Act of 1996
FMFIA – Federal Managers' Financial Integrity Act

G
GMLoB – Grants Management Line of Business

H
HFFI-FA – Healthy Food Financing Initiative – Financial Assistance Program

I
IDA – Individual Development Accounts
ILR – Institution Level Report
IPERA – Improper Payments Elimination and Recovery Act

IPIA – Improper Payments Information Act of 2002

N
NACA Program – Native American CDFI Assistance Program
NMTC – New Markets Tax Credit
NOFA – Notice of Funding Availability

O
OCFO – Office of the Chief Financial Officer
OFM – Office of Financial Management
OIG – Office of Inspector General
OMB – U.S. Office of Management and Budget

P
PAR – Performance and Accountability Report

Q
QALICB – Qualified Active Low-Income Community Business
QEI – Qualified Equity Investment
QLICI – Qualified Low-Income Community Investment

S
SECA – Small and Emerging CDFI Assistance

T
TA – Technical Assistance
TLR – Transaction Level Report